Gypsy Wind Speaks

Gypsy Wind Speaks

Life Lessons from a Sailboat

Coy Theobalt

Library of Congress Control Number:		2016905012
ISBN:	Hardcover	978-1-5144-7656-7
	Softcover	978-1-5144-7655-0
	eBook	978-1-5144-7654-3

Print information available on the last page.

Rev. date: 04/04/2016

To order additional copies of this book, contact:
Xlibris
1-888-795-4274
www.Xlibris.com
Orders@Xlibris.com
732852

CONTENTS

PART THREE
The Other Side of the World

PART FOUR
Back in the Islands

PART FIVE
Everything Changes, Everything Ends

APPENDIX A

APPENDIX B

This book is dedicated to Kevin Maddock, my dear friend and fellow boat captain.

His direction, support, challenge, and humor were imperative in my living my personal dream.

We all miss you like crazy. Cancer may have taken your life but not your spirit.

Thanks for all the tough love.

Acknowledgments

There are so many people that have supported my insanity over the years. My thanks go to Tim Lane for getting me back on the water; to Capt. Barry Graves for having sold me a fine boat; to Greg Geisen for your friendship and encouragement; to Paige, the bartender at the Elysian Resort, for being a great friend and listener to my stories and rants; to Cindy Shearer and Kevin Maddock for giving me a place to come to when I thought I was going insane and for great grilled cheese sandwiches; to Mike and Karen Miller for their friendship and many gallons of great coffee; to Jordan Barrows for joining me in the journey and becoming more than just a friend; to Paul Drda for your humor and lighthearted approach as well as your ability to fix anything; to Paul Jefferson for teaching me about the fine art of bumbledicking; to Derek Kellenbeck for your story in the book and being one hell of a first mate; to Gary Garner for your friendship and the use of your island car; to Fred Melton for inspiring me to finish the book by your writing.

I would also like to thank my children, Coy Austin and Morgan Elizabeth, for loving your old man in spite of himself and supporting his lifelong dream.

Thanks to Nell Davis, my former spouse, for your support and encouragement to "do it while you are still able."

To Charlie, the love of my life, for keeping my ass in the chair long enough to finish this project.

I would be remiss if I didn't thank Jeanne Uphoff Anderson, my first editor, for keeping me on track and reminding me I wrote it for my grandchildren.

Finally, I salute the great folks at Xlibris Books for holding my hand through the process.

The Day I Became a Sailor

For a number of years, people would hear me chatting about my time on the water and ask, "So you're a sailor?" I'd hem and haw and say, yes, I sailed and that I loved sailing. But it was very hard for me to actually reply with certainty, "Yes, I'm a sailor."

My resistance to this declaration comes from the many books I've read about the adventures of sailors around the world. Real sailors were those who had faced death and destruction many times, only to emerge from the cold salty waters beaten but ready to live another day. *Those* people were sailors, in my mind. A "person who sails" is someone who takes his boat out on a pleasant and benign day, weather-wise, and sails back and forth across the lake while enjoying a favorite beverage. On the other hand, sailors are made of grit and salty air, with hands callused and red from the wind and sun.

The day I truly became a sailor started out as a routine outing on Santa Barbara Channel just off the coast of Southern California; we were planning a four-day trip around the Channel

> The day started out as a routine outing, riding the wind across Santa Barbara Channel.

Islands. The channel is only about thirty-five miles wide, and according to my sail plan, we'd be in a safe harbor in five to six hours. It was a beautiful day, with the *Weather Channel* reporting eighteen to twenty knots of wind and five- to seven-foot seas—a perfect day for a sail with two crewmates. Tim Lane was a novice like myself, and Greg Geisen was a complete rookie.

We motored out of the Santa Barbara Sailing Center in a relatively new thirty-two-foot Hunter sloop—one mast, basic rigging. We had gone over the pretrip list in the morning over strong coffee and bagels. Tim made our lunches before heading out so we wouldn't need to be below deck any longer than necessary. Our sail plan called for us to motor northwest from Santa Barbara for about an hour and then turn due west and set our sails so we could ride a nice leisurely breeze across the channel.

All was well as we unfurled the sails one by one and felt the surge of the boat underneath us as she picked up speed. The best sound in the world to a sailor is when you turn off the engine and hear the wind in the sails. We set our course of 285 degrees west-northwest, trimmed the sails, tidied up the boat, and sat back to enjoy a great day on the water.

To this point in my sailing career, I had traveled a maximum of fifty miles in a day across open waters without being able to see the destination, and this trip was much shorter. We could make out the high hills of Santa Rosa Island in the distance.

As we sailed along, we chatted about the physics of sailing, a subject that continues to fascinate me the more I'm on the water. My buddy Greg asked the typical questions, like "How can we go into the wind and yet go forward?" I began to notice the swells getting deeper as we talked, but I had no worries at that point, as the little sloop glided up and down with ease. My thoughts returned to physics. Did I mention this happened to be Greg's first experience sailing?

About two hours into the trip, the wind picked up, blowing from twenty to twenty-five knots. This is a perfect wind speed for someone who sails often, but I noticed Greg's knuckles turning a shade of blue white as he gripped the side of the cockpit. The boat was heeled over (leaning over more in the wind) than he was comfortable with, so I gently eased the line that controlled the mainsail, and the boat took a more upright position on the water.

After making this adjustment, I saw that the ocean was looking more menacing. The swells were deepening, and the wind had increased once again. It was blowing close to thirty knots. I realized at this point Tim was reaching for the deck bucket, not to swab the deck but to use for other reasons. He was greener than the sea, and the look on his face said, "This isn't a good thing."

By now, the sea swells had increased to the point that when the boat reached the bottom of the swell, all we could see on either side was a wall of seawater. The wind really began to howl, and I started thinking about what we should do next to keep ourselves on course and safe. My crew, by then, couldn't go up to the front of the boat and accomplish

> All we could see on either side was a wall of seawater.

what I thought would be the next best steps. So we decided to drop the mainsail completely and try to get at least one sail tie on the back of the boom to hold it in place.

The next few minutes of this trip are when I realized I was indeed a sailor.

I looked back toward the coast of California to see nothing but a sky filled with sea salt as the wind blew the tops of the swells off into the sky. Looking forward, I saw the same thing. We were twenty miles offshore and eighteen miles from our destination. My assessment of my crew: Tim was so seasick he couldn't walk, and Greg was scared out of his mind. I told them that we were going to be okay, but we had to continue toward the islands rather than turn back. I told them that I needed them to stay focused, do as I said, and hang on. We found life preservers and jack lines to keep us from being thrown overboard.

I'll never forget that moment when I stood at the helm of that boat and made the choice to continue on.

The sea raged in gale force winds above forty knots, and the swells were fifteen to eighteen feet high. With my eyes filled with salt, I started the engine. Then I turned the boat into the wind as we motored up the side of a huge wall of green water. As we approached the top of the swell, I released the line that held the jib sail and yelled to Greg to crank it in with the winch as fast as possible.

At that point, the worst thing that could have happened *did* happen. The line got caught on a forward part of the boat, and the pressure on it was too strong to free it, so the sail was trapped against the mast. This was dangerous in a howling wind. I managed to release the tension on the line holding the sail just as we reached the top of the next swell. The sail filled with air instantly and sent the boat screaming down the next wave nose-first into the bottom of the swell. As the boat buried into the swell, I screamed for everyone to duck, as a wall of ice-cold Pacific seawater came racing down the deck and across the cockpit of the boat. I looked up afterward to see Greg clinging to his tether and Tim with his head buried in the deck bucket.

There *was* good news. The impact of the swell freed the line that was caught, so I could furl in the jib sail to the point of creating a small patch of sail that we used as a storm sail to keep the boat's bow on track in the rough seas.

I let go of the breath I'd been holding—for something that seemed like an eternity. At last I had the boat back under control.

With some hesitation, I let myself believe that we would make it through this very challenging day. With the motor running and only a small bit of sail catching the wind, the ride became easier as I steered the boat at angles up one swell then down the other side.

We were taking it one step at a time. It seemed to take forever to cover those remaining miles. Eventually, I spotted land in the distance. Sure enough, it was the vague outline of Santa Rosa Island looming above the horizon. My shoulders began to release the tension that had built up over the past few hours. As we got closer to land, the sea loosened its grip on the boat, and we steered into a safe harbor.

When we set the anchor and tidied up the boat, I looked at my watch. We had been on the water for almost nine hours—nine hours that changed my life forever.

To me, a "life-defining experience" means one that allows you to see yourself and your world somehow differently, that gives you more clarity about yourself and your relationships to the world around you. That winter day on the waters of the Pacific Ocean was certainly one of those times in my life.

Today, when someone asks if I am a sailor, I say, "Yes!" without question, while at the back of my mind, I recall that perilous day many years ago.

> I believe that my time on the water and following the wind has made me a better man.

For me, sailing is the most exhilarating experience in the world. It requires you to rely primarily on the wind to take you to worlds unknown, whether you are crossing the Santa Barbara Channel, Caribbean Sea, or the Pacific Ocean.

When I'm sailing, my entire world becomes focused on only what is at hand, in the moment. I've learned more life lessons from my sailing experiences than from any traditional teacher. Those lessons have occurred on every level, from purely physical experiences to the more subtle spiritual awakenings that have transpired over the years. I believe that my time on the water and following the wind has made me a better man.

I invite you to share my accounts of life lessons that I have learned while sailing aboard both my sailboats, *Island Girl* as well as my beloved

Gypsy Wind. Both spoke to me, but *Gypsy Wind* held the strongest voice, so she gets first naming rights. I trust she will speak to you as well. You may never sail the seas of the world on a sailboat, but I am sure you'll find these life lessons very applicable in business, family, and all other matters in life. So sit back, relax, and enjoy the ride!

Capt. Coy Theobalt
December 18, 2015

Gypsy Wind sitting at anchor in Lindbergh Bay, US Virgin Islands.

Ithaca

When you set out on your journey to Ithaca,
pray that the road is long,
full of adventure, full of knowledge.
The Lestrygonians and the Cyclops,
the angry Poseidon—do not fear them:
You will never find such as these on your path,
if your thoughts remain lofty, if a fine
emotion touches your spirit and your body.
The Lestrygonians and the Cyclops,
the fierce Poseidon you will never encounter,
if you do not carry them within your soul,
if your soul does not set them up before you.

Pray that the road is long.
That the summer mornings are many, when,
with such pleasure, with such joy
you will enter ports seen for the first time;
stop at Phoenician markets,
and purchase fine merchandise,
mother-of-pearl and coral, amber and ebony,
and sensual perfumes of all kinds,
as many sensual perfumes as you can;
visit many Egyptian cities,
to learn and learn from scholars.

Always keep Ithaca in your mind.
To arrive there is your ultimate goal.
But do not hurry the voyage at all.
It is better to let it last for many years;
and to anchor at the island when you are old,
rich with all you have gained on the way,
not expecting that Ithaca will offer you riches.
Ithaca has given you the beautiful voyage.
Without her you would have never set out on the road.
She has nothing more to give you.
And if you find her poor, Ithaca has not deceived you.
Wise as you have become, with so much experience,
you must already have understood what Ithaca means.
Constantine P. Cavafy (1911)

Part One

Starting at the Beginning

How This Book Came to Be

In the fall of 1963, when I was eight years old, my father took me to Louisiana. He just picked me up at school, and we headed out. He neglected to tell my mother about this road trip, and to be honest, I don't think he had planned it either. It was the kind of idea that came to him when he was in one of the manic phases of his life.

But he was prepared, in his fashion. He had a fresh fifth of Ancient Age whiskey under the driver's seat, a new pack of Winston cigarettes, and a bag of peanuts. We left our hometown of Hot Springs, Arkansas, and headed south.

As he drove and sipped, my job was to navigate. It was during these adventures that my love of maps developed, and I read every detail on them as we drove. There were two reasons for my personal map quest. One was that I didn't want us to get lost. The other was to break the unbearable silence. Dad kept his thoughts to himself, and driving gave him time to sort it all out and make sense of life.

Eventually, I learned that the purpose of our adventure was to order seafood for the new business he was opening back home. At that time, I didn't really care why we were driving around the swamps of Cajun country. I just loved to go places with my dad. It gave me a chance to see him in another light other than standing at the butcher block in the kitchen of our family-owned restaurant.

We arrived at Tony's Pizzeria in the French Quarter of New Orleans about midnight. The late hour didn't stop Dad from going in the back door to greet his friend Tony and order a pizza. It was the first time I'd ever seen my father eat pizza, and it may have been my first time as well. He and Tony laughed and drank and told stories over sips from his bottle of Ancient Age.

> Little did I know that this odyssey would inspire a lifelong desire.

Little did I know that this whirlwind, whiskey-induced, manic-driven odyssey would inspire a lifelong desire deep within me. The second day of our trip, Dad hired a guy to take us deep-sea fishing out of Grand Isle, Louisiana. Our day on the water was slow and hot and not great for fishing. Dad mostly sat and sipped, smoking his Winston's down to the filters. But there were other things that took my attention that day. I was mesmerized watching the boat captain maneuver his vessel away from the dock and take her out to sea. He had lots of rope on board, which I loved, so the combination of watching him and playing with the rope was perfect for me.

My dream of driving boats started with that trip. Back at the dock, he showed me how a winch worked and how he used the windlass (a mechanical spinning gear used as a way to gain leverage to raise the anchor or other jobs on deck that demanded more muscle power to accomplish). The fish may not have been hooked, but I sure was.

That memory is as vivid today as my thoughts were then, all the way back to Arkansas.

I was fortunate to live in an area with five lakes within twenty miles of my house. When I started sailing at thirteen with my childhood buddy, Jim Pennington, I knew that someday I'd be a sailboat captain. I wanted to let the wind power my ship to ports unknown.

Like many childhood dreams, this one was placed on the shelf of my life after high school. I went to college like all my friends, got involved in life, and followed other passions that developed during that time. After flunking out of college my first year, I joined a singing group, Up With People, and traveled the world for a year trying to figure out what was next.

Returning to college was both frightening as well as challenging to me. After learning how to study and realizing I could learn like everyone else, I became an honor student. When I finally finished college after a rough start, it was a big deal. At that time, I was only the third person in our family to go to college. Learning how to study and realizing I could learn, I set out to make my mark in the world.

I married my college sweetheart. We moved to Denver so I could attend graduate school, adopted two children, moved to Tucson, Arizona, and divorced a few years later. My childhood dream of sailing was slipping further down my list of priorities. It was never forgotten—only delayed.

In the late nineties, I married again. She was a delightful woman who supported me fully in all my endeavors. And then came the day in the summer of 1998 when I informed her my buddy and I were going to California to get our sailing certifications. This caught her by surprise—we'd never talked about my dream until that day. I told her the story about my dad and our crazy trip to Louisiana and my fascination with the boat captain.

My dream began to come alive as we sailed around San Diego harbor.

My buddy Tim Lane and I set out for a week of living aboard a thirty-foot sailboat in San Diego. We had a great instructor and began to learn the ins and outs of sailing. My dream began to come alive as we sailed around San Diego harbor, tacking back and forth. Whenever I was driving the boat, I thought about the fall of 1963.

For the next several years, we sailed often. We leased boats from Florida to California and sailed in Mexico and the U.S. Virgin Islands. Every time, my dream would emerge from its slumber and be rekindled. It was during these days on the water that I started cogitating on the idea of becoming a sailboat captain as a vocation more than simply recreation.

After returning from one of these trips, I told my wife I was totally serious about becoming a captain and starting a sailing charter business in the Virgin Islands. I showed her a picture of the boat I wanted to buy. She was stunned, to say the least.

After several weeks of conversations, she said, "If this is what you really want to do, you'd better do it now while you're still physically able." I was about to pursue a forty-three-year-old dream! I'll be forever grateful for her unwavering support in my adventure.

This book is my personal odyssey of living that dream—and experiencing the nightmares—that are part of the journey. I learned so much, and that wisdom has served me well.

My hope is that this book will encourage you to live your personal dreams and that some of the life lessons I picked up along the way will serve you as well.

The Calling

The ocean calls.
The ocean calls me.
The ocean calls me to itself.
The ocean calls me to it. Selfishly I shy away.
The ocean calls me to it selfishly. I shy away without looking back.
The ocean calls me to it selfishly. I shy away. Without looking back, I follow.
The ocean calls me to itself.
The ocean calls me.
The ocean calls.

Sunset on the Caribbean Sea

The Journey Begins

Sitting on an American airlines flight to Miami, hung over from the party thrown in my honor last night in our home, my dream is coming to life. My wife dropped me off at Denver International Airport at 6:30 a.m. I'm wearing a fishing shirt covered with good wishes and the signatures of my friends. As we fly over New Orleans and start to cross a corner of the Gulf of Mexico, I stare out the window at nothing but endless blue ocean and blue skies. It's surreal, as is my life at this moment.

The time has come for leaving everything that has meaning to me to live a crazy childhood dream of captaining my own sailboat. I've been consciously working on this idea for many months, and the time has come to make this dream come true.

My wife thinks I'm crazier than a teenager on crack, but she is supporting my dream. Amazing. As tears stream down my face, I'm filled with overwhelming joy, fear, excitement, frustration, and renewed energy. I haven't felt so alive in a number of years. I'm actually living my dream. How many people get to do this? Very few, I think.

When we land in Miami, I head straight to the Mojito Bar for one of the best drinks in the world to get a little hair off this dog from the previous night's party. It's time to celebrate the dream becoming reality. I am alive and living my life fully. "This is going to be a successful adventure," I tell myself after finishing off the second drink and head for my next flight to my new seafaring life on St. Thomas, U.S. Virgin Islands. What lies ahead for me at this point is mostly unknown, and that is part of the excitement building within me.

I take in the view of the moon rising over the hills and declare this to be my new home.

I sleep during the flight and wake just in time to see the lights of San Juan, Puerto Rico, out the starboard side windows. Ten minutes later, we are wheels down at Cyril King International Airport on St. Thomas. I anticipate this to be one of many landings and takeoffs for years to come in the islands.

Stepping out of the plane and onto the black tarmac, the moon rising over the hills brings tears to my eyes. I inhale fully and declare this to be my new home. The warm Caribbean breeze brushes my face as if to say, "Welcome to de islands, Mon."

My dear friend Kevin Maddock picks me up at the airport, and we head to a little dock in French Town where he keeps his skiff. He directs me to stash my gear behind us so it doesn't get wet on the ride across Gregory Channel to Water Island where he and his wife, Cindy, have lived for the past two decades.

They moved to Water Island to flee the crazy life in Philadelphia where Kevin worked as a full-time bartender and carpenter and was more often than not, drunk. Kevin's life changed when Cindy and some caring friends intervened in his life. Kevin has been sober for many years now and is actively involved in Alcoholics Anonymous and continues to attend daily meetings. In fact, he has become the regional director for AA in the Caribbean.

When we arrive at their home, we're greeted by Hoot and Gibby, their island dogs, and Cindy, who promptly makes me one of my all-time favorite sandwiches, a semi-burned grilled cheese, cooked to order—a perfect meal for a hungry adventurer who needs some of the comforts of home.

Upon arriving on Water Island those many years ago, Kevin built a "tree house" for them to live in. Since then, they worked on their main house and just finished it before I arrived. They were unable to completely leave their beloved first "house" and decided to split time between the two. They live and sleep in the tree house and have meals and socialize on the deck of the main house. It feels wonderfully strange and surreal sitting on their immense deck overlooking Sprat Bay while watching baseball on television and seeing shooting stars at the same time.

After a short conversation, realizing I am falling asleep in the deck chair, I excuse myself for a much needed good night's sleep. For the past few weeks, I have been waking up in the middle of the night, reanalyzing everything that was happening and asking myself why in God's name I was doing this.

Waking before dawn, I walk out on the deck and sit quietly looking at five cruise ships lined up waiting to enter the harbor to release thousands of pasty white tourists for a day of jewelry shopping and bargain-hunting for T-shirts.

Across the Caribbean Sea, I catch a glimpse of the lights of St. Croix thirty-seven miles to the south. I imagine what my life would be like, living alone on a sailboat one hundred yards off shore and two thousand seven hundred miles from home in Denver, Colorado.

"Life is either a grand adventure, or it's nothing at all."
–Helen Keller

The adventures, friendships, heartaches, and life lessons I anticipate are preempted by a mixture of profound excitement with a healthy splash of fear added for good measure. I ask God for guidance through whatever lay ahead of me. Sitting there in silence, I could not begin to imagine what was in store for me over the next years, but I remember the words of Helen Keller: "Life is either a grand adventure, or it's nothing at all."

And I believe this is going to be by far the grandest adventure of my fifty years on the planet.

Overwhelmed with Beauty and Glitz

Kevin and I drop Cindy off for work on the waterfront in downtown Charlotte Amalie this morning in his Boston Whaler and head straight for some good coffee. Kevin seems to know all the great coffee spots, as well as everyone on the island. He nods knowingly to fellow AA members and chats up the lady behind the counter at the coffee shop. After breakfast, we head to the east end of the island. He drops me off at the Elysian Resort where I'll be staying for a couple of days until my new boat, *Island Girl*, becomes officially mine.

It's too early to get into my room, so I stow my gear at the front desk and walk to the Ritz-Carlton Resort next door. I'm blown away by the beauty and elegance of the place. Everything seems bigger than life itself. Being a country boy originally from Arkansas, I have never seen a place more beautiful or majestic.

The resort sits on top of a hill looking over Great Bay on the east end of St. Thomas, U.S. Virgin Islands. When I walk out onto the veranda, the first thing I notice is how incredibly blue the water looks against billowing cumulus clouds hovering over St. John's Island to the east. The second thing I notice is one lone sailboat in the bay. It's *Island Girl*. It's hard to imagine this will be my home and the Ritz will become my backyard. I stand there stunned at the beauty of everything around me.

I spend some time wandering around the property, checking things out. Every few minutes, someone from the hotel passes me and bids me "good day." I begin noticing the guests as I make my way down through the resort to the beach. This is where the "beautiful people" go on vacation, I think to myself. Feeling as out of place as a turtle on a fence post, I become extremely self-conscious about my clothes and my cap that's stained with sweat from fly-fishing the previous summer. Even my

> Even my flip-flops are not the right brand. To say I am uncomfortable would be an understatement.

flip-flops are not the right brand. To say I am uncomfortable would be an understatement.

When I arrive at the beach, my new boat is sitting high on the water. People are lounging everywhere, drinking sweet cocktails served by a mix of West Indians and other types of young people dressed in white shorts and dark blue shirts with the Ritz logo. They look perfect; me not so much. More like someone dropped there from a redneck kegger party.

Making my way down the beach, I begin feeling a little more comfortable. The folks down here are wearing similar clothes to mine, except for the stained cap. I walk over to the beach shack and introduce myself to Gloria, a sweet Puerto Rican woman with a beautiful smile. She says she's heard from Captain Barry about me (the owner of the boat I'm buying) and that she is looking forward to working with me. I take this as a good sign.

Gloria tells me Captain Barry has gone to town and will be back later. I thank her and head back to the Elysian to process all I have taken in over the past sixteen hours. It's overwhelming. I get my gear from the office, put it in my room, and fall across the bed, still amazed I'm here. I feel like pinching myself. The nightmares of trying to make all this happen have taken an emotional toll on me, but that is overpowered by a deep feeling that this is exactly where I am supposed to be.

I can't wait to see what's next.

Getting My Feet Wet

After a good night's sleep, I call Barry; he invites me to come to the Ritz-Carlton to be his mate for a half-day charter. It will be one of his last and my first. Barry is a soft-spoken man with a deep tan and kind eyes. He greets me on the beach with the dinghy; I can only guess it will become one of my primary modes of transportation in the years ahead. When I step onto the deck of *Island Girl*, I feel right at home.

Barry shows me around and then says he needs to go to the beach to pick up our guests for the trip. Sitting in the main salon of my new boat, I'm excited and terrified at the same time. With Bob Marley singing "No Woman No Cry" in the background, my eyes dart from object to object in the boat as I try to absorb everything. I say, "Yes!" out loud to my new life. I still can't believe what is happening, that my notion of running a sailboat charter company is so close I can feel it.

> I say, "Yes!" out loud to my new life. I still can't believe what is happening.

Barry returns with the guests, and we fumble our way through the charter. I feel totally out of place. Wherever I move on the boat seems to be in someone's way. But with Barry's patience, I slowly start to get more comfortable. I give our charter guests a lame version of a safety talk. Barry kindly adds the four or five things I forget.

During our sail, it's obvious to me that Barry Graves is the consummate professional in his demeanor and presence. Once we get the boat under sail, he starts talking about the islands and proceeds to give a geography, history, and sailing lesson simultaneously. I listen in slack-jawed amazement, finding myself feeling envious of his grace and knowledge.

At some point during the charter, he offers me the wheel of the boat. I hesitate but step into the helm. Feeling at home at last, I instantly start steering the boat across the swells of the Caribbean Sea. After a beautiful sail and snorkeling trip, we return to Great Bay, in front of the Ritz-Carlton Resort, which will be my address for hopefully years to come.

Barry takes the guests back to the beach. After returning to the boat, we debrief the charter, a habit that looks like something I should quickly develop with my own mates. He gives me pointers, encourages me to learn all I can about the islands, and then offers the best advice anyone could give me—he says it would be better if I would speak less and allow the guests to direct the conversation. It's his gentleman's way of telling me to shut my pie hole!

The other great piece of advice from Barry is to slow down, relax, and take my time when maneuvering the boat in tight quarters. Notes taken. It's a conversation taken to heart. The life lessons begin my first day on *Island Girl*.

Life lesson: Speak less, listen more.
Life lesson: Slow down, relax, and take time when maneuvering in tight
  places.

Island Girl in Great Bay off the east end of St Thomas, USVI

All Is Not So Well in Paradise

I will be forever thankful to Barry for his assistance and patience as he guided me through all the ins and outs of getting a business started in the Virgin Islands.

After a day of getting more comfortable on the boat and sailing around the islands, soaking up as much local history as Barry could dish out, it was time to get the business side of the proposition going. Barry offered to drive me to the various agencies I needed to visit to get the licenses and certifications to legally do business on St. Thomas as well as with the Ritz-Carlton Resort.

At first, I wasn't sure why he offered to help me. I'm a big boy and can figure things out for myself. But I must say, trying to do business in the Virgin Islands is about as easy as me winning the Nobel prize in literature.

After coffee, the first place we visit is the business license office, which is located behind the hospital in a nondescript building with poor signage. I would never have found this place. A petite woman dressed for success greets us and says we are in the right place, but we must first go to the Department of Planning and Natural Resources, better known as the DPNR, to transfer the boat registration to my name.

So off we go in Barry's island car. It's a late eighties Ford something or other, with bald tires and rust around the wheel wells. The paint is at least fourteen shades of blue that comes only from years of sitting in the Caribbean sun. The seats have rips, and the innards are fully exposed. It has trouble starting from time to time, but the air-conditioning is cold, and that's all that really matters. As it turned out, Barry's car was the nicest vehicle of any of my friends' "island" cars over the next few years.

Now, you should know that getting around downtown Charlotte Amalie, which is the largest town on St. Thomas, is like trying to make your way through the jungle with a machete. On any given day, there are as many as twenty thousand tourists wandering the streets in search of gold jewelry and shirts to take back home. St. Thomas is the cruise ship capital of the Caribbean and can host as many as seven floating Disneylands at one time in port. It's totally crazy.

Barry knows all the backstreets to get through town and out to the airport where the DPNR is located. We park, go inside, take care of business, and head back to the office behind the hospital. When we arrive at the government office and present the change in registration, the lady says it must be notarized. Great. Why didn't she tell us this earlier? The answer is an island thing. "Because you no ask" is always the response when you ask a *why* question of someone in government. (West Indians do not offer information that is not requested. Period, end of discussion. It was a lesson I needed to learn quickly to avoid multiple trips to the same place.)

I politely ask the government lady if there is a notary in this building. Of course not. She directs us about a mile away to the office of a lawyer who is just leaving for lunch as we arrive. So we decide to eat and return to his office later, where we get the paper notarized, pay him $10, and head back to the offices.

When I present all the papers, she asks me to give her the name of my business. I tell her, "True North Sailing Adventures LLC," which is the official name in Colorado. She tells us to wait and disappears behind closed doors. Twenty minutes later, she informs me that I can't use that name because it's too close to another "True North such and such." I can't believe what I am hearing. So Barry and I sit there in the waiting room writing out possible names for my business.

The process is the same every time we offer her a new name. Mind you, we have been at this task for better than five hours, and it is the first day of what already feels like a mind-numbing odyssey. We finally settle on a set of letters that don't spell any word. She likes that just fine.

After Barry drops me back at the Elysian Resort, I leave my paperwork in the room and head to the beach bar. I plop myself down at the bar as a large West Indian fellow emerges from the kitchen of Robert's American Bistro. He asks me what I wanted, and after looking over the drink menu, I say, "Surprise me." A huge grin spread across his face.

A couple of minutes later, he slid a concoction across the marble-top bar. After some banter, he said, "It's called Total Confusion, my signature drink." After laughing at the name of this creamy chocolate-looking beverage for a moment, I took a sip. As the saying goes, my world has never been the same. When he saw that I was more than pleased, he introduced himself as Paige.

Paige would become one of my best buddies and closest allies on the island. Since that fateful afternoon, I end up spending hundreds of hours in his presence. He called me Captain Cody. For some reason, he could never get that my name was Coy. I have cursed and blessed everything from my first bad charter experience to the teams in the Super Bowl with my friend Paige.

Paige is one of those real-life characters who remind you of a cartoon character, and to me, he will always be a West Indian version of Homer Simpson, at least in looks, right down to his body style! From his large belly that lapped over his belt to the shape of his head, he was a ringer for Homer in appearance. But other than Paige's tendency to be moody, the similarities in the two characters stopped there. When Paige spoke, he was articulate and very thoughtful, and he had a tremendous sense of humor if he wasn't in one of his "moods."

After two of his chocolate concoctions, I wandered down the beach and dropped into one of the resort's lounge chairs to ponder the day. Waking two hours later in the dark and having no idea where I was or how I got there, I sat dazed in the beach chair and remembered the two drinks. After slowly regaining my bearings, I made my way back to my room, promptly fell asleep again and didn't stir until the warm Caribbean sun was shining through the patio doors on my face the following morning.

I sat up in bed, cleared my head, and thought about another day of adventures with the local government.

Learning to Work the System

Everything changes when you move someplace after visiting as a tourist. Now you're just another local, and the tourist charms begin to subside rather quickly. When you decide you want to start a business in a foreign country, that charm you so fondly remember from your last vacation becomes nothing more than an old faded Polaroid of times gone by.

Such was the case as I renewed my quest for the paperwork to make my charter company operational.

Barry picked me up again the next morning. We stopped for at a local coffee stand in the town of Red Hook called Lattes in Paradise. My first experience of the dark roast coffee, swirled in hot foam, caught my attention immediately. I asked Barry where these folks were from, and he says, "Maybe Oregon." No wonder the coffee is so good!

Those of us who became addicted to the offerings of that little coffee stand coined a new name for it—the Crack Shack. I am not kidding when I say that every morning, hordes of people made their way to the shack. It was not long before I too succumbed to the addictive quality of their coffee. We all decided the reason we could not go a day without our fix was because the owners of the place put small amounts of some addictive substance in with the beans as they were ground—well, it *seemed* like it was that addictive!

It wasn't long before I befriended Mike and Karen, the owners of the Crack Shack. They were indeed from Oregon and had returned to the islands after spending time on St. John's working at an eco-resort called Maho Bay. They had gone through some of the same trials and tribulations that I was experiencing with getting a business started, so we commiserated as well as schemed together on how to work in this environment. They were a few steps ahead of me in the process, so they became another great source of how to deal with the crazy-making governmental structure on the island.

After my second latte, Barry and I headed out for another daylong adventure of dealing with the West Indian bureaucracy. I needed to pick up my new business license that I'd applied and paid for online. You don't do that at the same place we had been to the day before to get my trade name license. You must travel to an area of the island known as the Sub Base—where the U.S. Navy built a submarine base many years ago. No longer needed for this reason, the base was turned into government services buildings. The long, narrow sets of barracks housed everything from the agriculture department to the food stamp office. I had done my homework before moving to the islands by using the St. Thomas government Web site to apply for my business license.

When we arrived, a number of women behind the glass partition were chatting away about something. They were laughing and making all sorts of gestures with their hands and bodies. It proved quite entertaining, but they were not helping me at the time. After about ten minutes, I stuck my head around the corner and asked if this was the place to pick up my license. They said yes and informed me they would come to get me in the waiting area in due time. So Barry and I continued to sit and wait.

Eventually a dark-skinned woman with a beehive hairdo and dripping with gold jewelry motioned for me to enter her "office." She was parked behind a standard-issue gray metal military desk piled high with stacks of papers and manila folders. On her desk were pictures of family as well as pictures of herself in carnival regalia waving from atop a flatbed truck. I eventually learned she was one of the Queens of Carnival, an event that occurs during the winter months on St. Thomas.

She asked what she could do for me. I began explaining that I had applied and already paid for my license online through their Web site. She looked at me for a second and then started to chuckle. When I inquired as to what was so funny, she said they don't process online applications for people until they actually show up in person. I was thinking, *Welcome to the islands.*

I wasn't sure what to say. As I sat there, she started pecking my name into an ancient computer terminal.

"Later" to a West Indian is like "someday" to an American.

After about ten minutes, she located my online application. She asked her cohorts where she might locate this application and was directed to another three-foot-tall stack of papers and folders on a nearby desk. She exhaled strongly, and said she would have to find it in there somewhere, pointing to the pile, and we should come back later. "Later" to a West Indian is like "someday" to an American.

So Barry and I decided to eat lunch. Two hours later, she said she had not had time to look into the matter and to come back another day. When asked what day, she said she would call me when she found it.

After not hearing from her for several days, I decided to call her. When I reached her, she sounded like she had no idea what I was talking about, so I filled her in on our previous meeting and that she said she would call me when she located the file. At that point, I was assuming she had been busy with other matters and would get right on it, and of course, she would call me when she retrieved the data.

After several more days of not hearing from her, I called once again—same story, different verse. She promised me that she would begin in earnest to look for the file. After breathing deeply, I ask to come to her office the following day and get this taken care of. She agreed to a 10:00 a.m. meeting the next day.

When I arrived the following morning, right on time, she motioned for me to sit in the waiting area. An hour later, she called me in. Her first words were—and I am not making this up—"How can I help you?" After gathering my jaw from the floor, I took a deep breath and started explaining that I had been here a week before, that we had talked several times on the phone, and that we had a meeting this morning scheduled at ten to look over my application. After pausing, she said—and I am not making this up either—"Come back this afternoon after lunch, and we can discuss the issue." I thought I was going to explode, but I bit my tongue, turned, and walked out with Barry. Barry turned to me and smiled while mouthing the words "island time."

When we reached the car, I lost it. I started cursing the ground this lady walked on as well as the island we were standing on. After my tirade, Barry suggested we get some lunch and a cold beer and talk it over. It seemed like food and cold barley beverages were quickly becoming a form of therapy for me.

During the next two hours, Barry explained the island way of doing business. He was calm and patient and empathetic as he explained to me that nothing happens in a hurry in the islands. Nothing! And that to try to make things move faster is futile and will ultimately lead to insanity on my part. He also suggested I be a little more personal, a little less business-like with her. After nine seasons in the islands, he was delivering the same speech to me that I eventually offered to numerous others in the coming years.

With two beers, a burger, and fries from Tickles Bar at Crown Bay Marina and some of Barry Graves' wisdom under my belt, I was ready to face the island government once again. When we arrived, she motioned for me to enter her office. When I walked in, I greeted her and started asking questions about the people in the pictures on her desk. She transformed before my eyes! She lit up and became more animated as she pointed to a picture of a couple of smiling teenage boys and told me about her grandsons playing in the finals of a cricket match. After I spelled my name two more times, she started looking through the pile on the desk behind her.

Something had shifted in her demeanor. She appeared to look in earnest for my file. After another ten minutes, she pulled a manila folder from under a huge pile and opened it. I saw immediately that it was my application with a check from my bank in Colorado attached to it!

She proceeded to tell me once again that they don't do online applications before the person comes to the islands and that she would be happy to start the process now if I would like. I asked her how long this might take. She thought for a minute and told me a couple of weeks or more, depending on how much work was ahead of my application.

I sighed and asked her to do her best to expedite the process, as I needed my license to start working legally with the Ritz-Carlton. She said she understood the situation and would work to help me as quickly as possible. I thanked her profusely and offered to take her out sailing with her family whenever they wanted to go. She and the other women in the office looked at each other and started laughing out loud.

I asked Barry why they laughed when I offered to take them sailing. After *he* finished laughing, he explained that West Indians are generally afraid of the water and would never even think of going sailing. I was dumbfounded at this news! Culture shock was taking a foothold in my psyche at that moment.

I thanked Barry and told him that the coaching he'd given me had proved helpful—to always engage in a relationship topic before a business topic if you want to get anything done here. He was right. I told him how the lady had morphed into a different person when I asked about the pictures. Barry smiled and said something about my "starting to get it" as he headed out into the sea of Mid-American trinket seekers from the cruise ships, slowly making our way back to the east end of the island.

After ten days, I decided to check on the status of my application. The response was all about how busy things had been around the office—someone was out on holiday (the West Indian way of saying "vacation"), another out on maternity leave, blah, blah, blah. She said she would try to get to it in the next week. I was crushed and mad.

The following morning, as I was lamenting about my dilemma to one of my new friends while at the Crack Shack, she suggested sending a bouquet of flowers. I couldn't believe what I was hearing! That was bribery, in my book. My friend said if I wanted my application, this would help get it sooner than much later.

I gritted my teeth, borrowed Barry's ride, bought $25 worth of flowers, and headed west to the Sub Base. I couldn't imagine just walking in and handing her flowers, so I entered her outer office and waited until someone who worked there came by. I asked them to give the flowers to her for me. She smiled, and I bolted for the door.

I decided to stop at Crown Bay Marina Marine Store to look for some rigging parts I needed before heading all the way back east. While I was looking through a bunch of shackles, my phone rang. Sure enough, it was my friend informing me that my application had been approved and was waiting for me at the front desk. Amazing, to say the least!

Over the years, I learned that anyone in the government who had the power to hold up your business from daily operation was very fond of flowers and even fonder of fruit baskets! I never waited more than a couple of days to get anything I needed from that point on. The local flower shop and fruit stand adored me

Life lesson: Sometimes you have to play by the local rules to get what you need, even if it goes against your ethics.
Life lesson: Persistence pays off!

Solitude: Despair and Freedom

After getting my license, it was time to start making money. But for the next eight days we had unusually strong winds and ocean swell. As you can imagine, this makes the charter business difficult. When tourists see the high wind warnings and small craft advisories, they cancel planned charters or don't book one in the first place. So I've been alone for about a week in a small, secluded bay that protects me from the northeast swell and the forty-five-knot winds that are howling in my boat's rigging. It's also been raining on and off every day, so I open and close the hatches on the boat at least fifteen times a day to keep the stifling humidity from steaming me like veggies in a colander on a hot stove.

This break in the business has given me a chance to ponder my life. I've been going through many changes since I moved to Latitude 18. The salt air and the warm breezes somehow are turning my brain to mush. My ability to think logically and somewhat with my "American drive-forward brain" has become more of an "islander-mañana brain." The longer I'm in the tropics, the more my sense of urgency is falling by the wayside. Things that used to seem so important are falling down my list of priorities. I think Jimmy Buffet was right about "wasting away in Margaritaville."

My solitude has caused me to experience moments of utter despair and immense freedom. Very paradoxical.

I've experienced incredible mood swings from profound sadness and depression to times of great joy and excitement during these first few months down island. I've begun to realize how much I depend on interactions with other humans. I can see I've actually been grieving the loss of constant interactions with people. This is a wonderful and incredibly difficult thing for me to face.

In the midst of being alone, I've met some wonderful people. Jean-Marc and Susan from Montreal have been here in my cove for a few days. They're taking an eight-month sabbatical from the corporate world to just sail and hang out. Ken and Judy showed up last week. They're also from Denver! What a small world. We know some of the same people. Ken just bought a boat from a charter company and is on his "shakedown" cruise for a month with two friends. All these people have made my life richer and more fun than they will ever know.

I've been doing some reading. The books *Longitude* and *Planets* by Dava Sobel are totally fascinating. Her other book, *Compass,* is another great read that helped me appreciate the courage (or stupidity) of people who took to the high seas in the 1400s in search of the New World. They have my utmost admiration. I'm also reading Jimmy Buffet's *A Pirate Looks at Fifty.* Very engaging reading! So much of it sounds familiar to me.

This entire boat is still a wonder to me. I find myself living in a space of less than four hundred square feet surrounded on all sides by water and one hundred yards from the shore. My "car" is a seventeen-foot fishing skiff powered by an old and somewhat unreliable forty-horsepower Tohatsu outboard motor. My closest friend is a very large barracuda that lives under my boat. I have named him BB King.

I rebuilt a bilge pump and worked on the battery system this week. Both were challenging. I'm more grateful every day for a father who taught me not to fear mechanical things and to undertake any task with wonder and interest. Thanks, Coy Sr., for that good stuff.

Life lesson: Appreciate friends.
Life lesson: Learn to enjoy being alone without being lonely.

Waiting Forever

Interested in developing your patience skills? If so, waiting in line in the islands is something you should experience. It didn't take me long after I moved to the U.S. Virgin Islands that I began to notice something unusual, to my way of thinking. My father always said people should never have to wait in line to pay for something, and that became my mantra as well.

People of the islands view this a little differently. To a West Indian, standing in line is akin to a cocktail party in the States. It's a place where people catch up on what's happening with the grandkids or getting an update on someone who's been ill. It's a social hour. And I do mean hour! On average, over the years I lived in the islands, I never spent less than thirty minutes standing in line to purchase a $3 bottle of dishwashing soap.

> All the locals were smiling, interacting with folks they hadn't seen in a while. All the tourists appeared miserable.

At first, I was like all the other tourists at the Tutu Park Mall, where the local Kmart store is located. I was furious about the time it took me to check out. Didn't they know how important I was? Didn't they understand that I had places to go and things to do? After a few weeks of waiting, I began to notice something. All the locals in line were smiling, interacting with folks they hadn't seen in a while, or had just met at that moment. On the other hand, all the yachties and tourists appeared miserable. They stamped their feet, rolled their eyes, and cursed to themselves or anyone who would pay attention.

"The show" is what locals call it when neurotic tourists start to come apart at the seams. This could occur at any point, place, or time. I've seen grown men and women have complete meltdowns in line at Kmart! I've seen people throw down their cosmetics and comic books, and others run from the store screaming about how crazy these people are for taking so much time to chat with one another during checkout. Don't they know that you do *not* engage other people in small talk, especially the checkout person, when you are queued up to pay and get on with your busy and important life? Don't even get me started on the lines at the bank! I have spent more than an hour in line waiting to get my debit card back because the ATM decided to eat it for lunch. An hour! Sixty minutes of my life wasted in line.

What a life lesson it was for me as I started to simply watch what was happening and notice my own guts churning like I had just downed a huge plate of pig knuckles from the mall food concourse. (I'm not making this up. Pig knuckles! And by the way, they're awesome with a side of fungi (pronounced *foongy*)—which is a concoction of okra, corn mush, and spices.)

Sometime during the months I stood in line, it finally dawned on me that what Barry Graves had told me about doing business over beers when I first arrived actually applied to everything West Indians do. This was a huge cultural difference from my own life experience in the States. These kind-hearted folks were simply doing what they do, which is relating on a personal level *before* they do business. This realization was one of the greatest life lessons that kept me from going bonkers at the grocery or any other public place where people gathered in lines.

> After a few meltdowns, I began to realize that the local island residents understood something much better than I did.

Now, I'm not the sharpest crayon in the box; but when this "aha" hit me, I started to relax. I began to morph into an islander, to see time in line at the auto parts store or the budget marine store as an opportunity to breathe and connect with people. Soon I started looking forward to shopping for rolls of toilet paper and duct tape. I could stand in line with no other responsibilities for those minutes and enjoy "the show" in ice-cold air-conditioned space. What a gift these times became! I was transformed over time, and my life began to slow down. I started walking slower, talking slower, thinking slower, even eating slower. Everything in my life slowed down. It was wonderful.

After I had a few small nervous breakdowns and meltdowns along the way, I finally began to realize that the local island residents understood something much better than I did. They knew that developing relationships with other human beings is more important than doing business. What a concept!

When I'm back in America, I find myself torn between revving up my own internal combustion engine to the insane pace most of us live or allowing myself to remain calm and enjoy the moment. This recognition that I can set my own pace rather than allowing the culture to set the pace for me has been a godsend personally and, I believe, professionally. My blood pressure is lower, as well as my resting heartbeat.

I also think I'm emotionally healthier now. I would encourage you to think about the pace of your own life. Is it faster than you'd like? Do you feel as though you are running everywhere? Do you feel like you're "behind" most of the time? If so, take notice of your heart rate and your breathing.

And just stop! You can do it. Whatever you're doing can wait for a minute. Breathe. Allow your shoulders to drop. Take a few long, slow breaths. Walk a little more slowly. Try it on for a couple of days. See what happens. If it fits you, maybe you could become an islander as well, even if you never develop a taste for pig knuckles and fungi.

Life lesson: Relationship before business, always.
Life lesson: Slow down, breathe, and focus on the present.

Being versus Doing

When you live on a boat, most of your time is spent fixing something. Since I love to tinker, this is a perfect environment for me. I have a running list of all the stuff that needs repairs. Some have a "1" next to them, which means do it *now*, while others merit only a "3" or "4." Those are the little things like fixing the clock in my berth or picking up some new fuel filters next time I'm on land.

Life to me is sort of like my list. There are some things that need attending to right away, while other stuff can be put off for a while.

I need to return a call soon from my sister to make sure everyone is okay. But I can put off getting that annual physical until I return to the states in June.

Since I've been down here in the tropics, I've discovered another part of me that I am starting to think is just as important as getting everything on my list done. It's simply *being*. It's sitting quietly alone on the deck in the mornings, before the heat of the day, with no thoughts. It's *being* a part of the sunrise rather than watching it while making my mental lists.

> It's *being* a part of the sunrise rather than watching it while making my mental lists.

Being is something I'm not accustomed to, nor am I practiced at this way of living. When I was a kid, my mother used to describe me as "a nervous wreck going someplace to happen." I was in perpetual motion from the moment my little feet hit the floor until falling into bed at night exhausted. As I grew older, I was one of those folks who thought silence was something that needed to be replaced as quickly as possible with noise. I began to realize that being quiet was as foreign to me as a Junebug to an Eskimo. I was actually *afraid* to be quiet. Terrified might be a better word. I worked very hard to fill every moment of every day with some sort of noise, either physical or mental.

Let me tell you right now that this is no way for anyone to live.

Once I recognized that I didn't have any spaces between the notes of the music called my life, I understood why I always seemed to be out of breath, both in reality and metaphorically. So I decided to do an experiment. I was going to get quiet and stay quiet. My biggest challenge was shifting from being a human *doing* and began the journey of becoming a human *being*

I tried many different methods of getting quiet, from sitting cross-legged on the floor while reciting poetry to standing alone in the dark on one leg. Nothing seemed to work. As soon as I closed my eyes, my mind kicked into overdrive, reminding me of all the stuff that needed to be done. I could actually *see* my list as if it were right in front of me!

My next try at this project called meditation was to do it while running long distances—at least they're long for me. This was one of my healthier addictions over the years. So I thought that maybe if I could run, my mind would just shut off for an hour or so. Off I ran! I thought it was working until the day I stopped to wait to cross a busy intersection. While jogging in place, it dawned on me that I had been mentally rebuilding the carburetor on my outboard engine while running the past five miles. So much for meditating while running.

I started listening to recordings of great thinkers, and I heard someone talk about focusing on one particular object while meditating. This idea seemed to resonate with me. So (of course) I spent a few days thinking about what that object might be.

I finally settled on a lighted candle.

I'll always remember the first time I sat on a pillow in the dark before dawn, staring at a single candle. It was like magic. At first, my mind kept telling me how stupid this was and that I had much more important things to do than wasting my time doing this. But each day, it became a little easier to sit and simply stare at my candle. Over several weeks, I was able to allow thoughts that came into my mind to simply float on by. In other words, I was starting to lose my addiction to thinking. My mind started slowing down. I found myself breathing slower and deeper into my body.

The sheer terror of the thought of being quiet had left me! For the first time in my entire life, I started becoming totally relaxed. During my sitting time, which had increased to twenty minutes a day from about three at the start, not only was I *not doing something*, I was also actually *just being*—being a human on the planet who was sitting silently without his mind running wild trying to keep him busy enough to not have to face himself.

Then I began to have the experience of *becoming* the flame of the candle before of me. I was finally losing my mind and coming to my senses. Words

> I was finally losing my mind and coming to my senses.

are useless in expressing what I experienced. I lost all sense of me. My ego was finally being deconstructed to the point where all that was left was a person without needs, wants, or desires. My sense of "I" was dissolving into oneness with the cosmos. I was becoming a human being more than a human doing.

I've told people that learning to get quiet was the most terrifying event of my life. I thought I'd go insane if I got quiet (like that wasn't already happening) and that all the terrible events of my childhood would come rushing back like a mighty river breaking through a levee. I thought I'd start to remember all the mean things I had done to others that had haunted me since my teenage years. I fully expected to start remembering terrible, bad, and nasty stuff that actually never really happened.

But then, I realized that my mind *didn't* start dredging up stuff from my previous life. It just started to slow down. My mind started to take a breather just as my body was learning to breathe. For the first time ever, I was getting quiet. Initially, it felt like being dropped out of an airplane into the middle of a foreign country. I didn't understand the new terrain, nor did I speak the language, but it felt right.

I shed many tears in this process, but they were tears of joy, not fear or pain. I was becoming a whole person, waking up from all the years of being insanely driven by my mental inability to simply be quiet.

I've recommended sitting in silence to many people. Most say it sounds like a good idea, but few rarely start in earnest. Many begin but aren't willing to tolerate the internal criticism that their minds dish out for doing something as stupid as staring at a candle.

But this practice has transformed my life. My mind is much clearer. I've developed the ability to stop thinking about something, change gears, and focus on something entirely different. I'm much more reflective. I can sit in silence in a group of people and watch and listen rather than conjure up what I'm going to say next. And although I'm likely not the best person to judge this, I think I'm more compassionate and understanding of people's needs.

I am a better man. Just by learning to *be*. And "being" on my boat became better than I could have ever anticipated.

Life lesson: Don't just do something; sit there.
Life lesson: Learn to breathe into life and start to "be" versus "do."

Captain or Companion

Here in my quarters, I'm pondering the whole idea of what it really means to be the captain of this ship. It's more than merely directing a vessel through the water or standing on the deck describing the boat and her history to our guests. It's so much more. But what does it really mean?

The catalyst for this line of thinking comes from a couple of things. One is the book, *Tuning the Rig,* journal entries of Harvey Oxenhorn as he sailed on a one-hundred-forty-four-foot Barkentine Schooner from Boston to Disko Bay off the western coast of Greenland. A writer by trade, Oxenhorn describes his experiences in learning to become a sailor. Many of his entries involve George, the ship's captain, who is an even-tempered man who held the line on everything.

> At times, I'm paralyzed. But this is generated from trying to "make nice" for all those around me.

This "strong captain" concept has me thinking about my own style as the captain of a sailboat. My own fear of upsetting or disappointing others keeps nudging me. I see things that need doing or that I want done in a certain way, but I don't say anything. Why not? At times, I feel frozen when I really believe it's time to speak. I'm paralyzed. But this is generated from my internal self, my ego, trying to "make nice" for all those around me. I wonder if I am more of a companion on my own boat than a captain of it.

This comes to the surface most often when guests have extended stays on board. That's when I'm most handicapped. It's like some great hand is holding my throat and keeping me from speaking of things that need to be spoken. At least I *think* they need to be spoken. I'm so unsure.

There's another reason why I harbor these self-doubts. These times remind me of sitting in Mr. Yocum's seventh grade math class, realizing that I have no idea what he's talking about—and that at any moment he would turn from the blackboard, look directly at me, and ask me give my answer to the problem.

Today, well into my fifties, I know that feeling wasn't totally the fear of making a mistake but the fear of what my classmates would do when I got the answer wrong. I was fearful of the ridicule that only seventh graders can dish out, as well as being terrified that Polly Ann Chitwood would finally realize that I was as dumb as a stick and decide not to fall in love with me.

It's all those forces acting together that cause me to sweat and bite my fingernails. After twenty minutes of dread, Mr. Yocum turns, looking straight at me. Then as a hurricane turns from one island to another, his eyes shift ever so slightly, and I am saved. The spotlight is on Velma Whitehead. She answers the question. She is wrong. The boys start to snicker. She is mortified, but I am spared . . . this time.

This kind of fear has gripped me thousands of times. I hated school. But now I'm the captain of a sailboat, not some freckled-faced, red-headed, chubby kid in black Levis. I must start seeing myself as who I am and worry less about what others think. I must focus on what I know in my heart of hearts is best for the boat and my crew.

The major problem with this perseverating is that I am not absolutely sure what *is* best. So with my gut aching, I sit and wonder.

> I'm seeing that what happens right after a mistake is made is what makes a good captain.

Knowing what's best for a ship is much easier than knowing what's right and good for those who work for me. I don't want to make mistakes, but I'm realizing now, after months of being in the role of captain, that fearing making a mistake is actually the thinking that often leads to most mistakes.

I'm finally starting to see that making mistakes is human. Every captain makes mistakes and judgment errors. It's happened to every boat captain who has ever stood in the cockpit shouting orders to his crew. I'm seeing that what happens in the moments after a mistake is made is what makes a good captain. It's how quickly and calmly he goes about the business of midcourse corrections to minimize damage and save face among his crew.

The more quickly I recognize my errors and make the appropriate adjustments, the less damage is done to either my boat or my crew or my psyche. Admitting mistakes quickly and honestly without assigning blame is essential if I'm going to keep my crew believing in me as the master and commander of this ship.

Now it's time to get out of this bunk and get my crew busy doing some polishing on the stainless steel so the salty air doesn't eat the boat right out from under us.

Life lesson: Admit mistakes quickly without assigning blame or judgment.

Crazy-Makers

I've been on my boat now for almost four months. This season, I'm starting to get a wee bit crazy, I think. My mind fogs up and shuts down. I can't concentrate for any length of time without becoming irritated and fidgety. Sometimes I think I'm going nuts.

But then the phone rings, and a charter appears out of nowhere! I regain my mental balance, pull myself together, and perform for the people. It's not unlike the theater where we wait and wait for that special moment when the house lights go down and the curtain raises, and there we are, all alone before the audience. For me, it's in those times that we're fully alive.

Another crazy-maker is the physical problems that come with boat ownership. According to my current mechanic, my skiff motor has seized up. I'll find out today whether this means rebuilding the engine or replacing it altogether. Either way, I know it will be expensive. But I need that little outboard. I think not having it run for almost three weeks now is leading to my current insanity.

One week from today, I'll go home for a few days. I'm looking forward to seeing family and friends. It looks like I'll have to sell my truck to cover these expenses. I am once again reminded of the acronym BOAT: Break Out Another Thousand!

Speaking of going crazy, it hasn't rained for about three weeks either; the wind has been calm too, but I'm praying that tomorrow's forecast for rain is correct. I am ready for a few days of rain and wind. Not having wind to a sailor is like not having mustard for your hot dog.

> Perhaps today is a day of *being* rather than *doing*.

34

With all the crazy-makers around me, I'd like to be busy today, but I don't know exactly what I should be doing. Perhaps today is a day of *being* rather than *doing*.

Life lesson: When in doubt about what to do, stop, breathe, relax, and prioritize what needs to be done.

My "car" for transportation to and from the shore

Dare to Dream

Do you have what you want in life? It's been said that most people don't know what they want in life, but they are pretty sure they don't have it. I asked myself this question many times as I was approaching age fifty. I *thought* I did, but after closer inspection of my *true* wants, I realized there were a few things in this world that I dearly and passionately wanted before my departure from the planet. And one of those was starting a sailing charter business as a licensed captain taking paying guests sailing. And now I had accomplished that dream.

Island Girl was my first infatuation. When I first came to the islands, she was a perfect boat for me in every sense of the word—nice lines, manageable in size, and very roomy for a thirty-eight foot sloop and plenty of deck space for customers to enjoy.

But then another "woman" caught my eye.

Our love affair started so innocently. Whenever I passed the boatyard on the east end of St. Thomas, she gently called to me. After several months, I finally stopped to check her out; and within minutes, I was hooked. Everything about her spoke to me—the lines, her size, her beauty, the rigging, and her dark blue hull. I was lovestruck. I found myself climbing a makeshift ladder and standing at the helm holding on to the teak wheel. I imagined plowing through the sea with a group of excited guests on board. It was truly love at first sight!

So I set out to purchase my new love, a 1979 Formosa 51 cutter-rigged ketch sailboat. After several months of negotiating, filled with heartaches and elation, I was finally able to call her my own.

She measured fifty-seven feet from bowsprit to the stern rail and was more than fifteen feet wide at her beam. She weighed an amazing fifty-three thousand pounds, of which almost half was the lead in her

> Everything about her spoke to me. I was lovestruck.

keel. She was a blue water ocean cruising boat in every sense of the word and had a track record to prove it.

Her name was *Taihaku,* which I am told means "point of light" in Taiwanese. She was built by Formosa Yachts in Taipei in 1979 under strict supervision by her first owner. He moved from Sweden to the boatyard for a year to make sure no shortcuts were taken during her construction.

Once launched, he sailed her to Sweden. After several years plying the waters of the North Sea, she was sold and sailed to the Mediterranean Sea where she spent several years. A couple then purchased her with plans of sailing across the Atlantic to the British Virgin Islands to start a charter business. As the story goes, the husband decided on a new tack for his life and left his wife a week before they were scheduled to set sail.

Undeterred, she left Majorca, Spain, and single-handedly sailed *Taihaku* across the Atlantic. Three weeks later, she arrived on Tortola Island in the British Virgin Islands and started her charter business of taking people sailing.

When this woman tired of the chartering lifestyle, she sold the boat to Al and Mary Jo Thomas. They lived aboard and sailed her south to Aruba, Bonaire, and Curacao every summer to get out of the hurricane belt. When Al died, Mary Jo wanted to keep their beloved boat; but over time, she realized that *Taihaku* was ready for a new owner.

This was about the time I wandered into the boatyard and started my own love affair with the boat. As I was getting my financing together, Clarke, the boat broker, called me one day and said, "You're not going to believe this, but a guy from Las Vegas just walked into my office and bought *Taihaku.*"

I couldn't believe what I was hearing! After gathering myself, I told him that *Taihaku* was *my* boat and I didn't know what would happen, but somehow the boat would be mine. He certainly thought I was nuttier than a Christmas fruitcake and said he would keep me posted.

I was brokenhearted to say the least, but I kept telling my friends that this was not the end of the story. Sure enough, six weeks later, I received a call from Clarke. He said, "You're not going to believe this either, but the guy who bought the boat showed up with his family, and they wouldn't even get on it! After a couple of days trying to convince them that it would look better when the makeover was finished, he called me and said I should sell it."

I was ecstatic! Clarke asked me to make him an offer. I did, and the owner said yes. So I ended up purchasing *Taihaku* for $15,000 less than my original offer. To boot, he had already spent $27,000 on an engine rebuild, teak restoration, and a generator overhaul!

I could almost see Clarke shaking his head as he told me the good news. He said that in all his years as a boat broker, he had never experienced anything like this. I simply told him that I knew in my heart of hearts that *Taihaku* would be my boat sooner or later.

And now she was.

Life lesson: Trust your gut about your future and don't let obstacles
   deter you from your dreams.

TAIHAKU on the dock in Benner Bay the day I bought her

An Intermission
Torn between Two Lives

I purchased my new boat during the summer months. That meant I was in my home in Colorado. And now another summer has come and gone. The autumn winds are telling me it's time to head south for another season of sun, salt, and sea. The days are getting shorter, and the leaves are finally turning loose and giving up after a great fight to hang around. I have so much to do before I go, and I'm not quite sure where to start.

If you're like me, you often know what you should do, but don't do it. I know what healthy foods to eat, and yet I still order fried chicken. I know how important exercise is, and I still sit in front of the television instead of taking a walk or going swimming. I know that I should take my medications on time, and I consistently "forget" to take them. What am I going to do with myself?

I'm coming to the realization that the answer is in the question. I want to think that I am Mr. Fitness or Mr. Eat-Right. But the grim reality is that I am neither of these guys. I'm more of a Mr. Wish. Why I'm this way puzzles me. I have all the knowledge anyone could want on these issues. But that doesn't seem to change anything. I can watch my weight creep up the scale all the summer and sit and think that it would be a really good idea to get out and get some fresh air.

Now, when I'm working in the islands, my life is different in many ways. I eat right, exercise every day, get plenty of sunshine and vitamin D or K and whatever other letter I'm supposed

> I get up early and watch sunrises. I meditate more than I medicate.

to have. I get up early and watch sunrises. I meditate more than I medicate. I pay much more attention to my body and what it tells me. I'm more self-sufficient. In a nutshell, I am healthier overall.

So why there is so much disparity between my two lives? I really don't know. I remember that last spring I was looking forward to "doing nothing" during the summer. I was tired, sunburned, and my body ached from all the physical activity it takes to run a charter boat. But this past summer was one of the busiest ones I've ever experienced. I was on the road every other week working with men with cancer, teaching them the solitude and joys of fly-fishing. My wife also had lists of "honey-do" jobs that kept me running when I was at home and off the road. Now I'm tired, sunburned, and my body aches from all the physical activity it takes to run a nonprofit and be a decent husband. Go figure.

I find myself saying I need to get back down island for some needed rest and to refocus on the things that I value. Life is funny that way. I talk about being present, and most of the time, I think I am. But after this particular summer, I'm not so sure. I guess I really like the concept, but it takes too much effort to "be in the here and now." I'd rather lie on the couch and dream of playing in the World Series, making the play at third base that wins the game. Or maybe just sleep through all the glorious sunrises of the summer so I can get another hour in bed.

I'm disgusted with myself. I think I'll go out to the kitchen for another apple fritter and more coffee and then get back on the couch and imagine hitting a home run. Or maybe I'll get my butt in gear and get out there and enjoy the day. It's too early to tell.

Life lesson: Taking stock and personal inventory of life is essential to healthy living.

Part Two

Gypsy Wind Is Born

A New Name

During the summer, the new short-term owner had the boat moved out of the boatyard into a rather rundown marina in the cesspool on the south side of St. Thomas called Benner Bay. After returning to the islands for another sailing season to be with my new boat, I decided that my boat's name, *Taihaku*, was wrong for her new adventures. As she sat on the water in the boat slip, it occurred to me that she needed a new "pirate ship" name. After a night of many rum drinks with close friends (and exuberant offerings to Poseidon and Neptune), she was renamed *Gypsy Wind, Queen of the Caribbean Sea*.

Changing a boat's name is a sacred event. You see, we sailors are a rather superstitious bunch. So before risking the ire of the sea gods, I thought I'd better do some research about name changing by going to the greatest source on earth for that sort of stuff: Google.

I read many accounts of how to go about this process. The easy part is applying with the U.S. Coast Guard for a name change and sending them a check. The challenge was how to do this in such a manner that the gods of the sea, particularly Poseidon and Neptune, would smile upon my boat and me.

After much planning, I called on my best friends, Capt. Jordan Barrows and first mate Paul Drda, to help me. I explained my thinking, and they agreed that this surely must be done right. So we devoted the next few days between charters to preparing for the big event.

We searched the islands for just the right costumes as well as copious amounts of rum to satisfy the gods. We invited the right people to be aboard for the event.

Finally, the night arrived. We shuttled people from the beach out to the boat for a wonderful dinner. Then the festivities began.

We gathered on the foredeck of the boat under warm, cloudless skies. I asked each person to say a little something about the boat and their hopes for her future. Then as master and commander, I began a rambling but heartfelt speech about the history of boat name changing and the importance of the tradition. I explained how we had meticulously scoured the boat and removed any remaining signs of the old name, *Taihaku*. We had removed the wooden letters from each side of the bow and attached them to a small replica boat made of flotsam. (*Flotsam* is a fancy nautical term for "sea trash.")

Jordan, Paul, and I knew the best island sites for gathering flotsam if we needed something that was hard to find any other way. It's a sailor's version of dumpster diving. So *Taihaku's* replica was fashioned from gifts from the sea. Her hull was half of a ten-gallon blue water jug, cut lengthwise. Her masts were pieces of driftwood, her sails were scraps of cloth, and her rigging was made of nylon fishing net line.

At the proper time, we began the official ceremony. I said, *"For thousands of years, we have gone to sea. We have crafted vessels to carry us, and we have called them by name. These ships will nurture and care for us through perilous seas, and so we affectionately call them "she." To them we toast and ask to celebrate Taihaku."*

Then everybody raised their mugs and shouted, "To the sailors of old! To *Taihaku!*" and took a sip of rum. I continued: *"The moods of the sea are many, from tranquil to violent. We ask that this ship be given the strength to carry on. With a strong keel, may she keep out the pressures of the sea."*

Again, the mugs were raised, and the grand assemblage shouted, "To the sea! To the sailors of old!" And everybody took a bigger sip of rum. I concluded: *"Today we come to send this lady Taihaku to sea to be cared for and to care for this captain and his family and crew. And we ask the sailors of old and Poseidon and Neptune, gods of the sea, to accept Gypsy Wind as her new name, to help her through her passages, and to allow her to return with her crew safely!"*

And again, the raising of mugs—"To the sea! To the sailors before us! To the Gypsy Wind!"—followed by the biggest sip of rum yet.

After all this pontificating, we poured a cup of diesel fuel into the hull of the little vessel with the wooden letters TAIHAKU glued and duct taped to her sides. Then Jordan lit the replica on fire and set her out to sea. We had timed this event knowing that the tide would be heading out through a small opening between two islands.

As the voodoo vessel formerly known as *Taihaku* sailed around the point and out of sight, burning brightly for Poseidon and Neptune to see, my boat was officially christened *Gypsy Wind*. We all shouted her new name three times as I walked the deck from bow to stern and from port to starboard, pouring relatively expensive Mount Gay rum onto her decks and into the sea. We made many more toasts from years gone by to the present and future. It was an unforgettable night.

Gypsy Wind was now my new maiden, and I her lover. The next months and years would prove to be some of the greatest and most challenging years of my life.

Life lesson: If you are going to make changes, make sure you do your homework first.

(If you are interested in the specs on *Gypsy Wind*, please go to appendix A in the back of the book. I added it only for boat geeks like me that want to know such things.)

Gypsy Wind under sail

Homecoming

Somehow I never thought it would—or even could—happen. Oh sure, I expected it to happen in some sort of vague spiritual way but not in a reality sort of way. When I bought *Gypsy Wind,* I thought idealistically, "Hey! In a couple of weeks, we'll have her cleaned up and ready to sail!" Wrong! I purchased the boat in August, and now it is January, and we haven't yet hoisted the mainsail.

And then yesterday, the rigger who had been inspecting and repairing the standing rigging handed me an invoice and said, "She's ready to go sailing!" At first, it was like someone talking under water. With his New England accent, spoken through his burly huge mustache, it seemed ethereal. Did he just say that *Gypsy Wind* was ready to go sailing? I think he did!

I still loved her dearly, but the honeymoon was officially over. Now we needed to begin the daily work of growing together, and I needed to learn how to run a day sailing charter business. At this point, I had no idea how long this odyssey would last. As one of my best friends is fond of saying, "We'll know more when we find out!"

I'd been dreaming of the day her sails would fill with the trade wind breeze, and she'd begin to heel over as the mizzen, jib, and mainsail opened to the sky. But now I felt a deep dread. It was like being a little kid going up to that first house on Halloween—you want to ring the bell, but you're also a bit frightened at the same time.

Our first move was to get her out of the mangrove cesspool we had been living in for five months. I said good-bye to the dock master and tossed him the bathroom keys he'd loaned us. We bid farewell to the new set of live-aboard friends we'd made while enduring our version of *Jurassic Park.* I waved at Joe Cool, the man who resurrected my fridge and freezer, and to Patsy, the great cook at the little diner near the docks. (Patsy's meatloaf is as good as my grandmother's.) As we left the mosquito-infested hellhole, the phone rang. Gary, our neighbor, said he noticed we were gone and wanted to be sure all was well. Boaters are some of the greatest people on earth.

We moved the boat to Great Bay, that spacious spot on the east end of St. Thomas I'd enjoyed on Island Girl. The bay opens to the east, with lots of room for the trade winds to keep the bugs away. *Gypsy Wind* was now sitting in her home (for the time being). We dropped the anchor in thirty feet of water, and she settled back on the anchor like a baby snuggling with her blankie. At last, she could breathe (as well as myself and first mate). We sat on the foredeck and watched the sun set over the Ritz-Carlton and the moonrise over the island of St. John. It was magical.

The following day at 2:00 p.m., I made the first call from the helm of *Gypsy Wind* to hoist the mizzen sail. We pulled up anchor and motored east into bigger waters and farther away from folks watching for our possible sailing blunders. Then I made the call to "ready the mainsail," which took my three crewmembers about twenty minutes. Trying to figure out the lines on a sailboat with four separate sails can be like trying to find the correct exit on the 405 freeway in Southern California, a crapshoot at best. But then the call returned: "Ready to hoist, Captain!" The mainsail was ready. I gave the call to hoist. As I stood at the helm and watched the sail unfurl, I wasn't totally surprised to find myself moved to tears. All the work that we had done on this beautiful vessel was at once worth every minute of blood, sweat, tears, and cash.

Next, we attempted to unfurl the jib sail—until its halyard broke. (Notes taken.) We finally unfurled the staysail and sat back with cold beers to celebrate the moment.

Gypsy Wind had finally been returned to her rightful place on the open waters of the Caribbean Sea. It had been more than four years since her sails were filled with the salty air. I think she smiled as we slowly lowered her sails after three hours on the water. We turned her bow into the wind, dropped the mainsail, and left the mizzen sail flying so everyone could see that *Gypsy Wind* was home again.

Life lesson: Persistence pays off.
Life lesson: Always invite your friends to share in your excitement about something.

Boat Rats

For a number of weeks, all was well on the boat other than the daily work of cleaning, sanding, repainting, and polishing stainless steel. Then one day, things started getting weird. I'm not sure exactly when it began—when things started moving around on the boat. First, it was a little rubber duck my wife gave me to remind me of her while I was sailing. Then it was a little figurine of a sailing ship and then a votive candle and some other small things. We blamed it on the spirits. Yes, we decided, the spirits of the former *Taihaku* were amusing us aboard the *Gypsy Wind*.

It wasn't long before I decided to find a more practical answer to the dilemma. The logical answer was that my first mate, Paul, was playing tricks. He was the type who would do this. So when I confronted him about it, he said that he thought I was doing the same thing to him! After I made him swear on a stack of nautical charts that he was not the culprit, we agreed that further investigation was necessary.

After a few days, it became apparent, through "gifts" we found scattered about, that it wasn't boat spirits on board but a rat. An honest-to-goodness rat! So we began a process to eliminate him. Traditional mousetraps were the starting point, but they proved useless. I set out six different traps loaded with Cheez Whiz, bacon, peanut butter, and summer sausage. The rat had a veritable smorgasbord of delectable foods to choose from—all gone within a day, without a single rodent caught. Then he left cute little teeth marks on my favorite type of apple. As many sailors know, an apple is a real treat to have on board at sea. Now he'd crossed the line.

> The rat upped the ante; he gnawed through my treasured talisman necklace. That, in my opinion, was an act of war.

Then the rat upped the ante, moving to even more irritating exploits. He chewed the ends from both cell phone chargers and gnawed through my treasured talisman necklace. He left the frayed ends of it dangling in the sea breeze near my bunk. That, in my opinion, was an act of war.

We escalated the fight with glue pads, d-Con, and packets of rat "treats" that were supposed to make him thirsty and leave to find a drink. After several days with no signs of our adversary, we believed that we'd nailed him!

For the next few days, we cautiously checked the areas where he'd made his presence known. No sign was a good sign. A couple of nights and a couple of rum drinks later, we declared victory! We poured copious amounts of rum over the port and starboard rails in gratitude to the gods of the seas.

The next morning, Paul awoke to the sound of crinkling plastic. He yelled, "I saw him! I actually saw him! I was an arm's length from catching him!"

"Ratman" was back with a vengeance. He'd left droppings all around the galley and eaten another apple. So all our pleadings and toasts to Neptune and Poseidon were to no avail. We were back at square one.

Except . . . we now had an eyewitness to the crimes. We had a positive ID: our boat rat was about five inches long, excluding his twelve-inch tail. This is the stuff that tabloid stories are made of. I could see the headlines: "Giant Boat Rat Eats Sailors!" Now it was time to focus all our attention on getting rid of the beast.

At the next port, we walked into town to stock up on reinforcements for the battles ahead. "The Terminator" was our choice of weapons for this behemoth. The package said it was designed for "giant rats," so it became our next line of firepower. The lovely West Indian lady at the checkout counter wished us luck as we marched out on our mission— may Neptune and Poseidon be with us! We had finally come upon a poison lethal enough to end Ratman's life.

There was no rest for us until Paul and I developed a conscious strategy to target our adversary. We studied him until we began to see his patterns and likes and dislikes. It wasn't until we actually started *thinking* like a boat rat that we finally ended his adventures on the *Gypsy Wind*. We eventually resorted to using strongest rat poison known to mankind, and it did the trick.

Six weeks is a long time to live on a boat with a rat the size of an armadillo, in my mind. And so it is with the "little things" in my life that cause me frustration. Maybe it's time to start thinking more about these irritants and systematically remove them so that I may enjoy more smooth sailing in life! Taking the time to consciously recognize the things in our lives that are draining our energy and well-being is paramount in living a life that is less frustrating and more enjoyable.

Boat rats are inevitable in our lives. They live in the recesses of our minds. I think the key to ridding ourselves of them is to slow down long enough to recognize the fact that they are running amok inside our heads.

Our thinking is filled with boat rats that emerge as nagging and persistent negative thoughts that challenge our well-being. Sometimes we must get bigger ammunition to fight them, like seeking out the help of a trusted friend or perhaps speaking with a professional counselor. Whatever method we use, the bottom line is that we must remove these nagging little mental creatures and give them a proper burial, whether it be at sea or in the comfort of our study.

Life lesson: When you have "rats" on your "boat," make sure you do whatever necessary to eliminate them.

Celebrating with first mate Paul Drda after getting the boat rat.

Changes in Latitudes

I woke up early one winter morning to a white hot sun and a cool easterly trade wind. Everything seemed so right, and yet everything was so wrong. Nothing seemed to be working out despite the great foundation I thought I'd laid the season before.

I'd spent countless hours building what I believed were solid business relationships with resort employees at the Ritz-Carlton, and they had been the source of almost all my charters the last season. Yet here I was, just sitting and waiting for charters to materialize. And they weren't.

Every day, I'd ask myself what was wrong. The people at the resort's concierge desk said they just weren't getting requests for sailing charters. I had a hard time believing them. (But then they had said that their remodeling was supposed to be done by Thanksgiving, and I hadn't believed that either. My guess is it'll be done by June.)

So I sat. And sat. Then one day it dawned on me that perhaps it was time to stop sitting and move my operation to another part of the island—to a new latitude. It seemed like the hard work I'd done was now holding me in a place that was causing me to go broke. But could I leave the most prestigious resort on the island? That would be crazy. And to even *think* of moving to the west end of St. Thomas was insane. I'd heard that *nobody* wanted to work down there.

> Perhaps it was time to stop sitting and move to another part of the island—to a new latitude.

But honestly, I was tired of competing with the resort for day sail charters. *Gypsy Wind* was second banana every day to the resort's fifty-foot catamaran. And of course, their first priority was to fill their own boat, not to generate business for *me*. And finally it dawned on me—if "nobody" wanted to work the west end, then maybe there was an opportunity there for us!

So I decided to see what was happening in Lindbergh Bay. We sailed in on a twenty-five-knot blow from the east, topping out at eight knots boat speed on the sleigh ride "up island." I'd been told that the bay had terrible holding, but *Gypsy Wind*'s anchor found good sand with a little mud mixed in.

The first thing I noticed was the quiet. There was only one other boat in the huge bay. There were no jet skis, no children screaming, no kite surfers, no windsurfers, and no loud music from the beach bar. It was tranquil, still, and beautiful other than the occasional whine of jet engines as planes departed the island.

The first evening, we ventured to the Caribe Resort and a Mexican food restaurant called Fajita's. The staff was friendly, the food was good, and the margaritas were even better. We eventually found the beach bars at the other two small resorts in the bay. Nice people everywhere! I told my mate that we had some potential here, but I'd need to meet the general manager of the main resort in Lindbergh Bay.

My first experience with the GM of the Emerald Beach Hotel was interesting. His assistant said he was too busy to meet me that day. No worries, I said. I asked what time tomorrow would be good for him. After a few minutes, she returned to tell me he was busy through the end of next week. No worries, I said again. I asked what time the following Monday after next week would be a good time for him to meet me. She left again, and when she came back, she said he'd see me in about ten minutes. My father always taught me that persistence pays off.

When I finally met with Joel, the GM of the Caribe, the first thing I told him was that I wasn't there to be a pain in his ass. As he listened to the thirty-second version of my charter proposal, he seemed skeptical and with good reason. Here was this modern-day pirate asking him for access to his beach and his guests. He asked for a package of information. That was a good sign—at least I'd get at least one more meeting with him. In the ten minutes I spent with him, he never smiled once. This guy was playing tough and, as I said, with good reason.

> He never smiled once. This guy was playing tough and with good reason.

My first mate, Paul Drda—that's right, Drda. I always kidded him about needing to buy a couple of vowels for his name—and I promptly put a package together: insurance, captain's license, boat documentation, release of liability waivers, and pricing. When I delivered it, Joel didn't have time to meet with me. *Great*, I thought. I didn't get my second chance after all. Now what?

So we waited. While we did, we checked the beach bar for quality and consistency. It had both. The burgers were tasty, and the rum was yummy. Three days later, Joel saw us having lunch in his bar and said we could offer our flyers there. Victory! Of course, we still had to actually create said flyers and business cards for this new venture, but we were in!

In our first week, we had as many charters as we had booked in the prior two months. Everyone was warm and friendly. And they liked having conversations with us, which was a lot different from our experience on the east end of the island.

And the lessons from all this? I learned fairly quickly that, to make my business succeed, I needed to change course, to try something out of the ordinary and new. The other lesson was to get over my fear of failure, as well as preconceived notions that in many cases were less than true.

Letting go of my own ego was the hardest battle to overcome. As usual, it wanted to keep me safe, comfortable—and miserable. At this point in my life, those were the last things I needed.

What I needed was income, and I needed it now. My bank account was dwindling faster than a bunch of Rastafarians leaving a bluegrass concert. This ship needed to change direction so the business could continue. This decision was one of the most difficult ones I had to make while working in the islands. Everyone told me I was crazy to take my boat to the opposite end of the island, away from all the great snorkeling spots and cruise ship tourists. But sometimes you just have to go with your gut. Difficult times call for creative decisions that often go against the wind.

Life lesson: Persistence often pays off, especially when combined with compassion.

Life lesson: Sometimes we must change our course to get to the destination.

Sunday Mornings

We began our charter business in earnest after getting our flyers and business cards made. This end of St. Thomas is very different from the east end where I had spent the past couple of sailing seasons. The most obvious difference is fewer people and the second is more West Indians. This was a real treat for Paul and me. It was also across the street from the airport.

I awaken to the sound of the first plane out of St. Thomas, the 7:00 a.m. flight to San Juan, Puerto Rico. And it is only twenty minutes late—perfect for island time.

My Sunday mornings are a mixture of jazz, quiet time, and the smell of jet fuel. It's my own version of church when I'm in the islands. I turn on the radio, pour myself a cup of coffee, and ease slowly into my day. Several hours pass without speaking a word. I move more slowly, and I think much more slowly. Time is spent thinking about problems and working slowly to solve them. There is no reason to be in a hurry at all on these days.

Bumbledickin' is a good word for this. It's a word coined by my friend, Paul Jefferson, from Wichita Falls, Texas. He uses it when he has no particular chores to do that day, yet he wants to be in the garage or his workshop doing something to keep him out of the house. Sometimes it feels like a Southern version of ice fishing.

This morning has a little Hemingway quality to it. I could be sitting at anchor looking out over Havana, Cuba.

So I bumbledick around the boat. This morning the generator is holding my attention. It's been kind of funky-sounding lately, and then it simply stops without notice. We worked on it day before yesterday without success.

But in this morning's quiet, thoughts come more clearly as the jazz station plays classic tunes from the forties and fifties with nothing newer than 1970 today. This morning has a little Hemingway quality to it. I could be sitting at anchor looking out over Havana.

After further pondering, it dawns on me that I haven't checked the raw water strainer for ocean debris. Sure enough, a piece of plastic trash bag appears to be the culprit which I remove with the precision of a surgeon. Now the generator is purring away, like a cat being scratched behind the ears, charging my battery banks and getting the fridge and freezer cold again. Ah, sweet victory!

More pondering on this glorious morning leads me to thinking about what the generator is trying to teach me. The realization hits me that I have been unconsciously ignoring the problem for more than a week. I remember hearing the generator's engine changing tones and speed. But did I take notice and try to fix it or at least understand it? No. I did what I love to do—I pretended it didn't exist and that everything was fine when it wasn't. Thank God I didn't let it get to the point of damaging or even destroying the whole thing. (The other day, I read in some paperwork that the previous owner of *Gypsy Wind* paid nearly $10,000 for it! At this point in the journey—or any other—I do not need that expense.)

So on this glorious morning, I think about what I've just been taught. I reflect on all the problems in my life and how I ignored them—my first marriage, my kids' teenage years, and my own addictive stuff. I'm realizing that this is a most serious thing. What if I spent the rest of my days on the planet simply ignoring all the lessons life is trying to teach me? After all, you never see a hearse pulling a U-Haul. It's all here and now. So it's in my best interest to learn *all* I can *while* I can.

Life is full of these teachers. Sometimes I choose to ignore them as they wait in silence until I acknowledge their presence and welcome their lessons. "Okay," I think. "Bring it on. I'm ready. I think."

And while I wait for the teachers, I'll just pretend I don't hear the water pump running strangely, and then maybe I'll look for my dinghy that disappeared because I ignored the rusted shackle that attached it to the towing line. But before I do any of these things, I need another cup of hot jazz and a few more bites of Sunday morning.

Life lesson: Don't put off doing what needs to be done. Face the difficulties in life and address them.

Life lesson: Look everywhere for life teachers. You will find them if you only will look.

Looking from the beach bar at the Emerald Beach Hotel in Lindbergh Bay

Life as Improv

There's a rule in improvisational comedy called accepting all offers. It means you do whatever the audience suggests—whatever comes your way. The other day, my friend Dave Schrader and I were talking about using improv in our work, and he suggested that our spiritual lives are a lot like improv. The more I thought about his idea, the more I realized that it makes perfect sense.

God, life, the universe give us situations; the more we resist, the more uncomfortable and ineffective we become. However, the more open we are to "accepting all offers," the more creative and alive we become.

> The more open we are to "accepting all offers," the more creative and alive we become.

When pondering this, I realize that every moment of every day is a form of improv. We make stuff up as we go along the path of life. Every decision is either accepting or rejecting the offer before us. Saying yes to every offer doesn't mean agreeing with it. Rather, for me, it's an embracing of the process. Accept what *is* at this very moment. Don't deny, repress, suppress, or reject what *is*. I embrace it by saying yes.

Whenever feelings of being trapped or upset bubble up with me, most of the time it's because I'm resisting what *is*. I'm creating a myth about myself or my situation in life rather than opening myself to all the possibilities that the situation has to offer.

On the other hand, when I say yes and agree with reality, my life is not necessarily easier, but I'm congruent with what's in front of me at that moment.

In one of the opening lines of his book, *The Road Less Traveled*, Scott Peck says that "life is difficult" and when we finally start understanding and agreeing with this truth, then life gets easier. This is similar to the improv concept of accepting all offers. Once I say yes to what is before me, no matter how unpleasant, awful, repulsive, or crappy it might be, I can then be open to all the possibilities of what I can learn from the experience.

For me, today, life is not about getting and knowing, but it used to be. Many years of my life were spent wanting folks around me to think that

> This road isn't about getting and knowing but about learning and growing.

I had everything I wanted and knew everything about whatever I encountered in life. Somewhere along the road, I took a turn and started down a different path. And it was definitely less traveled. It was riddled with weeds and obstacles and difficulties of all sorts. But I've found it to be far more interesting and challenging than the road I was on before. This road isn't about getting and knowing but about learning and growing. I now try to see every situation in life as an opportunity to learn something about myself and to grow from it.

The old road was more about control and dominance. This road is way different. Now I'm realizing that the concept of control is an illusion. I can no more control life than cause the wind to blow whenever I wish. And the old way was so exhausting! The more I tried to control everything, including myself, the more out of control everything seemed to be. It was an insane way to live.

Now the realization of little or no control over anything sits perched in my psyche. And I consider that a good thing. Agreeing with reality and aligning myself with it causes life to get easier. I start to see life as more of an adventure than something to be conquered. Life is my teacher, and I am the student. Period.

When we start agreeing with life—or, as I like to say "what is"— anxieties, worries, and fear are less predominant, and I'm more relaxed and able to manage better in life situations. *Gypsy Wind* has certainly given me the chance to learn more about that.

I'm observing when my anxiety increases. It's when I'm imagining what things will be like in the future. My mind imagines running the boat up on a reef and how bad the damage would be to the keel. Then how much it would cost to repair it creeps into my psyche. What must be given up or sold to pay for it? My mind goes into overdrive when I allow this to happen! These are never good thoughts. I call this "awfulizing."

On the other hand, when I just stay in the "now" or with "what is," my blood pressure drops, my anxiety subsides, and my life is more manageable. My focus is on reality rather than fantasy. Doing what needs to be done *now* rather than fixating on how bad things could be tomorrow brings me peace of mind.

And things *may* be bad. I don't know. But when life takes me there, I can deal with it in the moment with the actual facts and figures versus my imagination. I can deal with it, no matter how unpleasant it may be. Imagining the future as being horrible is most folks' way of *seeing* their future. Unpleasant over horrible is much better to manage.

It's interesting to me that my imagination is partly why I am living my dream today on a sailboat in the Caribbean. Our own ability to create in our minds what it is that we want can *not* be underestimated, in my opinion. If I hadn't held the thought or image of myself becoming a boat captain in my heart all these years, this book about my experiences on the water would have never come to be. And furthermore, I wouldn't be learning all the life lessons that have come with this adventure.

So I'm off to learn what life has to teach me today. Good, bad, or ugly, it will be a grand adventure!

Life lesson: Stay present. Live in the here and now rather than in a fantasy world about the future.

Life lesson: Be open to what life is trying to teach us at every turn.

Letting Go of the Wheel

Teaching a fellow traveler is one of the best ways for life to teach us. I eventually sold my first boat, *Island Girl*, to a fellow from Colorado. Today I gave a sailing lesson to the buyer of *Island Girl*. Part of the sale was that I would spend up to a week teaching him all the ins and outs of sailing his new boat.

We were just off the south side of Water Island. The wind was blowing twenty knots from the southeast with five- to seven-foot swells. There was a haze in the air from Montserrat Volcano blowing its top five hundred miles down island. Great billowing clouds provided a beautiful canopy for the day.

My internal anxiety increased as the new captain attempted to steer his new boat in the ocean swells. My challenge was to be still and experience the new owner's inexperience as the helmsman of his boat. He was making sharp S-turns as he learned to anticipate the next swell coming up under the boat. He was doing what sailors call oversteering. It was almost impossible for me to just sit and allow him to learn. It's not easy watching anyone learn something that you can do without even thinking.

> My challenge was to be still and experience the new owner's inexperience.

Actually, it seemed to me that he was overthinking *and* oversteering. We swayed to port and then to starboard over and over. The sails filled with warm salt air and then flapped as the breeze came across the bow and then just as quickly filled in again. The rigging slapped and jerked as the boom swung back and forth. It was not a pretty sight. I knew that we weren't in imminent danger, but I admit feeling a bit embarrassed as I wedged myself into the cockpit to keep from being tossed around.

Island Girl has what is called weather helm. This means that the harder the wind blows, the more she wants to turn her bow toward the wind. This is a great quality in a boat but takes getting used to as a helmsman. The boat also has a wing keel, which is great in many sailing situations, but it creates a challenge when you're sailing across swells. The boat comes to the top of the swell and then wants to turn. The combination of the two forces can be daunting for a novice at the wheel.

My natural tendency is to step in, grab any problem by the horns, and correct it as quickly as possible. There's a time and place for that, but today was not one of those times or places. Still, I found myself reaching for the wheel and correcting the problems. As I calmly corrected his errors, it dawned on me that he was depending on *me* to fix things whenever we were going off course. He'd look at me as if to say, "Don't just sit there—do something!"

Remembering to tell myself that this day was about *him* and *his* need to feel the swells and that *he* needed to learn to turn the boat to counter each action with an opposing action. So as he continued to oversteer the vessel, I forced myself to sit quietly, looking out across the vast Caribbean Sea, tasting the salt on my lips gently advising him when to steer to starboard or port. All the while, as the boat swayed, I told myself, "Don't just *do* something—*sit* there."

> If I'd taken the helm, he wouldn't have learned nearly as much as he did by steering himself.

In that moment, I experienced what is often the case in coaching executive leaders. Taking the helm and steering us through the swells in a relatively straight line with far less turning and commotion would have solved the immediate problem. But if I'd done that, the new owner wouldn't have learned nearly as much as he did by steering himself. If he was to become a sailor, he needed to get the feel of his new boat under him, much like Barry Graves did when I first bought *Island Girl* from him.

Looking out at the other boats and people watching us, my own ego was getting excited at the center of all this. *My* ego wanted *me* to do the steering so there would be no stories told at the bar that night about the "two idiots out there trying to sail." Once again, I understood how many leaders "do" for others and derail the learning process because their own egos demand that they always look good in every situation.

Leaders in the corporate world often tell me when I coaching them that they could do a job themselves in less time than it takes to teach somebody else to do it. While that's certainly true, this creates two problems. One is that the employee isn't allowed to experience the learning process, and the other is that the subordinate continues to be overly dependent on the leader. And when these two things occur in business, everyone becomes increasingly frustrated and starts losing their self-confidence.

As the sailing lesson neared its end, I noticed that my student was starting to anticipate the next swell and steer away from it ever so gently. Our S-turns were slowly straightening out. It was rewarding to see him beaming with joy. I'm not sure that this is something many leaders ever see in their people.

Now when I'm coaching an executive, I hold the memory of that new boat owner glowing with the excitement as he learned to live his own dream. I think we could use a little more of that type of coaching in the corporate world.

Here's to learning to doing less and sitting and observing more.

Life lesson: Do less, be more. Allow the student to learn instead of trying to "teach."
Life lesson: Check your ego at the door when teaching others.

The helm and wheel of the Gypsy Wind

Another Tequila Sunrise

A few days later, we had a party celebrating the sale of *Island Girl* and the fact that I am once again a one-sailboat owner. I'm reminding myself once again that drinking cheap tequila is never a good idea, even with friends. I awoke at 3:00 a.m. with a screaming headache that can only be compared to having your head in a vice while someone pours hot oil on it. Not much fun. And I know better—I've been through this before on a number of occasions and every time promising myself that will not happen again. But here I am, scrambling around in the dark, praying that there is ibuprofen in the cabinet. I find it, down four tablets with a quart of water, and wait for them to do their thing. After an hour and a half, I finally get back to sleep.

Upon waking from my hangover, it dawns on me that life has livened up considerably in the last few weeks. We've turned our attention from repairing and restoring the *Gypsy Wind* to scrambling about with charters almost every day. The focus has shifted, but the intensity is even higher than when we were repairing the rigging.

Since we moved the business from the posh Ritz-Carlton, it's becoming more obvious that I never really fit in there. I pretended to, but that is an exhausting way to live. Now feeling more relaxed, I feel this is the place where I belong. The people we're working with now are generally hard-working middle-class folks who saved their nickels and dimes and came down island to escape the cold Midwest weather. They're salt-of-the-earth pasty-white men with well-developed beer bellies and women who are stout and sporting Wal-Mart swimsuits. I love these folks. Yes, I'm right where I belong.

> They're salt-of-the-earth pasty-white men with well-developed beer bellies. I love these folks. Yes, I'm right where I belong.

Our clientele is varied, to say the least. One guy retired from Chrysler after thirty-five years. Another repairs mopeds in New Hampshire.

Several married couples work together—one has a refrigeration business in the mushroom capital of the world, someplace in Pennsylvania. We've also had a national sales director for Mary Kay Cosmetics whose husband works on the space shuttle as a pyrotechnical engineer. We've taken a few very well-to-do folks sailing here, but their style is different from the typical Ritz guest. These people are more down-to-earth and friendlier. They made their money the old-fashioned way through hard work and sweat.

My wife left for Colorado yesterday after spending a week with me. I'm sad to see her go. She had a great week on the boat and loved steering *Gypsy Wind*. I think they may have started a love affair. She expressed my feelings perfectly when she said, "I feel so welcomed here on this beach and at the resort. At the Ritz, I always felt like I was trespassing."

Now I'm off to get provisions for today's charters. Time to get into pirate mode and have a fun day entertaining wonderful people who appreciate what I'm doing. What could be better?

Life lesson: Don't drink to excess, especially cheap tequila.

Today

Today is here.
Today is here now.
Today is here. Now what?
Today is here now. What will I do?
Today is here now. What will I do to savor it?
Today is here. Now what will I do?
Today is here. Now what?
Today is here. Now!
Today is here.

(This is a type of poetry style called "Nested Meditations" created by Kevin Anderson. They are meant to be read slowly, out loud, using the punctuation to create inflections that change the meaning of each line. The poem is mine)

An Invitation!

After a week of constant charters, it was time for me to take a day off. Here's an invitation to you: Come with me on my day today.

I'm standing in the town square listening to gospel music sung by talent from the local Baptist church, drinking a piña colada in the shade of a giant sea grape tree.

It's Sunday afternoon on St. John Island, and I'm acting like a tourist. It's great! I actually feel like a visitor today and bought some jewelry from Alton, a local West Indian friend. He wants to go sailing with his girlfriend next month. We chat, laugh, do a little business, and soon my friends and I are hiking to Solomon Beach.

The trail is dusty and covered with cactus. Yes, cactus because the U.S. Virgin Islands are arid. We get most of our rain from August through December and then comes cool, dry air for the next five months. It's delightful here, but on this Sunday afternoon, we're sweating as we walk along the leeward side of the island away from the cool trade winds. The nourishment of the summer rains is long gone.

Finally, as we round a corner, the stifling heat gives way to cool offshore breezes. We descend the hill toward the sound of breaking waves. Through the trees, I see at least thirty boats moored outside the swimming zone.

Solomon Beach is "clothing optional." Today, no one is exercising that option, which is a very good thing in my opinion. Most of the folks here today should never be seen nude in public or private! A large group of people ("large" in both senses of the word) have beached themselves and are burning to a crisp in the afternoon sun. Apple-shaped women with bright orange hair bounce in the waves, while men with decades-old beer bellies are sitting in the sand in their Speedo bathing suits, smoking and scratching themselves. It's quite a sight to behold.

We find a spot under a coconut palm, and I gather a couple of old palm fronds to make myself a comfortable place to lie down and nap, digging my toes into the cool moist sand. Two short hours later, the cool breeze wakens me as the sun starts its daily march to the horizon.

We gather our things to hike back to Cruz Bay. The air is much cooler now that the sun is setting. The light on the trail is the kind my photographer buddy, Jim Rae, calls "perfect." It casts

> The light casts long shadows. The boats in the harbor have a surreal look.

long shadows across the trail, and as we round the point, I see that the boats in the harbor have a surreal look to them, as if that same buddy with the camera had put the "beautiful" filter on the lens of my eyes. It's awesome.

We make our way into town to take full advantage of the happy hour prices at Woody's Bar. With a few more friends, we ease our way over to the shopping district. One person in our group wants to get some really cool jewelry, but after cruising three different stores displaying the coolest stuff I've ever seen, she walks away empty-handed. So much for shopping.

We dine at my favorite restaurant on St. John, Rhumb Lines. It's a low-key, laid-back, funky place planted in a courtyard surrounded by old buildings. I like being able to see the stars while eating. The owner is off tonight, but her husband is dishing up great Asian Fusion cuisine. I order the sesame-encrusted Ahi tuna—rare. It's done perfectly, as always. We all split a piece of key lime pie and listen to a local artist play her weathered Martin D-28 guitar. She sings folk songs, and everyone knows the words. I lean back in my chair and soak up every drop of the night.

We slowly return to the ferry dock for our twenty-minute ferry ride back to St. Thomas. In Red Hook, we meet up with more friends. After a nightcap, my friend Churchill, one of several

> There is a cool easterly breeze swaying my hammock. Soon the moon has fallen toward the sea to the west.

"gypsy" taxi drivers, takes us to the west end of the island. I climb into the backseat of his 1989 Ford Aerostar van and nap all the way.

Upon arriving at the Emerald Beach Resort, we make our way through the hotel lobby and down to the beach and release the skiff from its mooring to find our way in the dark back to *Gypsy Wind*, waiting patiently for our return. There is a cool easterly breeze gently swaying my hammock back and forth, and I learn a couple of new stars in the clear night sky. Soon the moon has fallen toward the sea to the west. I go back to my quarters and sleep soundly until morning.

A great day in the islands. I am blessed.

Life lesson: Take time to enjoy yourself on a regular basis. Spend a day acting like a tourist.

Island Bureaucracy

All is well aboard *Gypsy Wind*. Not.

At 9:30 a.m., the Department of Preservation of Natural Resources police boat approaches us. Three West Indian men with guns in their shoulder holsters tell me that the *Gypsy Wind* can sit in this bay on anchor for only fourteen days and then must leave for six months. Great! Just great.

Before starting my business here in Lindbergh Bay, I'd called the DPNR to see if there were any restrictions for anchoring in the bay. I was told that the only restriction was "no anchoring within two hundred fifty feet of the concrete wall on the west side of the bay." Great!

So now, I'm being told basically at gunpoint that we have fourteen days to leave and then can't come back for one hundred eighty days. That would be after the two busiest months for chartering. Great!

It's just another obstacle in paradise. I must trek out to the DPNR office at the airport and start what will undoubtedly be a very long, tedious conversation. Another life lesson looms on the horizon. Great!

In the meantime, I share my experience with John, the self-appointed keeper of the bay. To put it mildly, John is an unusual man. He has dark leathery skin, earned from swimming more than seven thousand miles in this bay in the last ten years. His teeth are stained from the constant cigarette he holds in one hand, and his mind seems pickled by the constant beer he holds in his other hand. He keeps his brews cold with an ancient "beer bra" that zips over the bottle. It looks as if it has held as many bottles as his swimming mileage. He likes the local microbrew "Blackbeard's Ale." So do I.

John was skeptical when we first anchored in the bay, but we've become friends. He coached my mate and me on where the moorings are located and how to moor our skiff so no one would trip over the shore anchors we use. John is very concerned about the welfare of others far more than his own.

> John tells me that the bay is the keeper of itself, that he is merely a participant.

Now John greets me every day with his crooked smile and curious black eyes. Despite his flaws, he is a delightful human being. When I asked him about his local designation as the bay keeper, he paused, took a long drag on his cigarette, exhaled through his nostrils, and told me, "The bay is the keeper of itself, I am merely a participant." When he said this, I realized that I had judged this man by his outer self and had come to the wrong conclusions. I must continually remind myself that wisdom is often spoken through the most unlikely characters. (Many thanks, Dan Millman, author of *Way of the Peaceful Warrior,* for teaching me this truth.)

So I started to ask John about his opinions and his life. He's multitalented, a Renaissance man in a Speedo and bib overalls. A sage in sheep's clothing, if you will. He's built houses, managed up to six projects at the same time, and served in the military. More recently, he's battled with the Port Authority to get the bay designated as a "no fly" zone. He tells me, "I'm taking a year off to regain my strength in the fight for the bay." He continues by saying, "I will never give it up." I know this is true just by the way he says it. I thank God that John likes me and has decided that I'm a good guy who cares for the bay almost as much as he does. Actually, I don't think anyone will ever care for this place with the same passion as John.

Getting back to my current problem, John coaches me about the DPNR. It's all about money. "Did they ask you for money?" I say, "Not this time." His response was "they will." He tells me that DPNR uses the bay to make extra cash under the table. I find this idea interesting and disturbing at the same time.

"Fight it," John says as he exhales blue smoke through his nostrils. He recommends talking to them, secretly recording the conversations. He touches the front pouch of his overalls, and says, "I always carry a tape recorder when I speak to them." His other piece of advice is to always get the name of the person I'm talking to. This is a lesson I'd already learned in dealing with any issue that requires action on the island. I know it has something to do with the culture but still not quite sure how.

John also recommends that getting my ducks in a row by looking up all I can on the Internet about Lindbergh Bay. Later, when I try to access my wireless connection, a message pops up telling me that my license to use my wireless device has expired and that I need to go to a Web site to renew it. And how am I supposed to do that if I can't get on the Internet? Great. Just great! Welcome to the islands!

Fortunately, we did *not* have to contend with the DPNR the rest of the season because the boat came out of the water shortly after our showdown in the bay. We left the bay ten days later to head down island to get *Gypsy Wind* out of the water for much needed repairs. But that is another story.

Life lesson: Take advantage of local knowledge when dealing with governmental issues.

Looking down on Lindbergh Bay

On the Rocks

This was a day I will not forget as long as I live. I'd always wondered what it would be like to be aboard a ship when she struck the rocks or an iceberg. Now I know.

We were taking a delightful couple from Memphis out for a half-day sail and snorkel. The weather was ideal. The wind was from the east-southeast at twenty knots. *Gypsy Wind* loves that much breeze. We headed out for our normal "three-hour tour." The southeast swell gave us an excellent opportunity to head to Saba Island just off the southwest corner of St. Thomas. The area around this island is known for great snorkeling and beautiful views.

We sailed for about an hour and then dropped our anchor in fifteen feet of turquoise Caribbean water. It grabbed the sand on the first try. Our guests had never snorkeled before, so my mate, Paul, gave them excellent instructions, and off they went. I stayed aboard the boat to make a few phone calls and spend some time alone. After an hour, everyone was back on board enjoying snacks and drinks, soaking up some rays, and having a great time.

> Everyone was enjoying snacks and drinks, soaking up some rays, and having a great time.

When it was time to pull up the anchor and head back home, the engine wouldn't start. After some unsuccessful tries and trouble-shooting, sailing off the anchorage seemed the best option for us. I asked Paul to partially raise the mainsail and unfurl just a few feet of the staysail to catch the wind and push the bow of the boat around so we could sail away.

There was a reef about fifty feet behind the boat. As we pulled up on the anchor chain, the boat began to drift directly toward the reef. I knew this could be big trouble.

The only way out of this situation was to pull up the anchor at precisely the same time the wind pushed our bow to starboard. This would take a coordinated effort. I shouted to Paul to raise the anchor just as the wind began to fill the sails. After several attempts, a favorable breeze, and some adjustments to the sails, *Gypsy Wind* began to move away from the rocks and into deeper water.

With shaking knees and white knuckles, we sailed away. This had been a close call, but luckily, our guests didn't seem to notice our anxiety and continued to enjoy the ride. I made a couple of humorous comments, and we all laughed as we went on our way.

As I think back, it was at this point that I began to make a few critical errors in judgment. I'm not sure if it was the near miss, the rum from the night before, or just plain stupidity, but what followed was the sort of experience that movies are made of.

I decided we could sail southwest from Saba Island out into the Caribbean Sea. After turning around, we would sail back, and our guests could take photos of this beautiful island. Then we'd have a nice beam reach sail back into our home port of Lindbergh Bay. Good plan.

There was another factor in this equation: the equatorial current or drift. This is a steady ocean current that moves ceaselessly from east to west around the globe near the equator. The east end of the island is protected from these currents by St. John and the British Virgin Islands, and because our normal tide surge is less than one foot, it was almost insignificant. But I hadn't had much experience with this current and its strength until we moved down to the west end of St. Thomas. This was different. We were also two days away from a full moon, which tends to increase activity in the ocean—including equatorial currents.

So I sailed *Gypsy Wind* out far enough (in my opinion and experience) to clear the island. We attempted to tack, which means steering the bow of the boat through the wind, but one of my guest helpers let a line to the mainsail go too early, and we stalled in the wind. No worries; we simply allowed the wind to turn the boat downwind, and we jibed, allowing the wind to cross the back of the boat rather than the front. In the time that it took to make these corrections—less than five minutes—the current had pushed us back to the north several hundred yards. This proved to be a crucial factor.

After the jibe, I set our new course to pass Saba Island. In minutes, I told Paul that I didn't think we could make it without tacking again. My new plan was to pass a small group of exposed rocks off the west end of Saba, sail behind the island, and then continue home.

I had a minute to breathe. The rocks seemed far enough off our port bow. Our forward progress wasn't what I wanted, so I called for more sail. Paul hesitated for a moment and then unfurled our Genoa, the largest one on the boat. Our speed increased instantly. Now I just needed to clear the rocks, and we'd be on our way.

> I just needed to clear the rocks, and we'd be on our way.

My heart is racing, and my palms are sweaty just thinking about what happened next. I'm ashamed to write this, as the next events are solely my responsibility. There is no one to blame but myself. My decisions, or lack of them, created a near-death experience for me and, more important, my guests and crew.

As we sailed eastward, the *Gypsy Wind* was being pushed to the north by the currents toward what's known as Dry Rocks. They are a series of coral fins sticking a couple of feet out of the water and are only about one hundred yards long with narrow openings between them. They look menacing to any sailor, and they surely did to me.

It was as if they sucked us into themselves. That's the only way I can describe it. One moment, I had them cleared, and the next I didn't. I started to steer up and away from the rocks, but I knew my boat would have stalled without enough forward momentum to tack and change directions. I looked off my port and saw that there wasn't enough room to turn that way either. In that moment of clarity, I realized that my boat and my life and my dream would be dashed on a small reef in the Caribbean Sea.

> We heard grinding and scraping of the hull of a ship on a coral reef—the absolute worst sound I've ever heard in my life.

I yelled for Paul to come on deck where he was making fresh drinks for our guests. He saw immediately what was just ahead of us. He ran and grabbed the life vests from the forward cabin. I told our guests that we were going to hit the rocks, but I'd keep them safe at all costs. We hurried them into their vests just as we heard the sound that no boat captain ever wants to hear—the bumping and then grinding and scraping of the hull of his ship on a coral reef. It's the absolute worst sound I've ever heard in my life.

The next few events kind of run together for me. The first swell that hit our starboard side pushed the boat over to port and slammed us against the jagged rocks. It sounded as if everything below deck broke loose. Anything not tied down flew across the boat and hit the port side of the cabins below. I cringed at the sound of breaking glass. When the next swell broke against the hull, I heard something crack like the sound of a large board being broken in two.

I knew I needed to get everyone safely off the ship. I ordered Paul to get into the dinghy and start the engine, and I helped our guests into it. As Paul's friend Sarah got in last, I handed her a gallon jug to bail water from the dinghy that was already almost full from being tossed about. I told Paul to take the guests to shore on Saba Island and then come back for me. Saba was about a quarter mile east of Dry Rocks. As they moved away, one of them called to me, "Godspeed!" That word and how he said it is forever burned in my mind.

I was now alone on *Gypsy Wind*. This beloved boat, part of my life's dream, was now being ground and tossed and crushed between the sharp coral heads jutting out of the sea. It was like being in a pinball machine. I was thrown back and forth across the deck with every swell that broke under the boat, slamming her broadside into the next coral head.

I knew it was time to make that hard call. Picking up my VHF marine radio, words I never dreamed I would say came out. "Mayday! Mayday! Mayday! This is sailing vessel *Gypsy Wind* located just west of Saba Island. We're on the rocks. I'm not sure I can save the boat. At this time we are not, repeat, not taking on water."

Here I was, telling everyone in the world that my boat was going down. I felt hot and sick to my stomach. The first offer to assist was from a boat just to my west. Then I heard more boats on the radio offering to help.

I have tears in my eyes as I remember this event. Boaters are the greatest people in the world when it comes to being there for others.

Then the coast guard asked me for my latitude and longitude, but I was too nervous to give them. Another boat told them my coordinates. The coast guard wanted to be sure all my passengers were safe, and I was relieved to tell them that they were off the boat in the dinghy with the engine running.

Fear is a strange thing. As I talked to the coast guard and the other boats, I tried not to sound panicky or terrified, but I know my fear was out there for the world to hear. It's hard to describe what goes through your mind at a time like this. I can't say that I felt real fear at that moment. Fear coursed through my veins just before we hit the rocks and then two days afterward, shaking uncontrollably with fear as I imagine what could have happened. I mostly felt a sense of deep respect for my boat and intense disappointment that I'd allowed all this to happen because of my errors in judgment.

I felt a tremendous responsibility to do whatever possible to save my boat. I remember telling her out loud through streams of tears that she had saved my life, and I would do everything within my power and ability to save hers. There was no worry about losing my own life—I could jump into the water at any time and save myself. But leaving the boat that I loved was not an option. I had invested so much time, effort, and money into her. She was my boat, and I was her caretaker. I had put her into this situation, and by God, I was going to do everything in my power to save her if at all possible.

> I would not leave the boat that I loved. I had put her into this situation, and by God, I was going to save her if at all possible.

Pulling myself together enough to assess the situation, I looked down into the bilge and saw that she wasn't yet filling with water—a very good sign. All my skill sets were needed to save her, but first I had to have a plan.

As I looked around, I realized that there were small openings between the rows of the rocks we were sitting on. *Gypsy Wind* could get through them at the correct angle, but she was sitting broadside to them. I also saw that we were now behind the rocks that were sticking out of the water. Apparently, when we'd hit those, the stern had swung sharply to port, and we actually floated between two rows of rocks. One row was now behind us off the stern, and the bow was stuck between the rocks ahead of the boat. With every swell, she was tossed back and forth between these rocks. She was moaning and creaking as we shifted from one rock to another. It was as if she was crying like a mother that has lost a child. It was an awful sound.

Gypsy Wind was hurting and in a lot of pain.

If we were to have any chance of getting through this ordeal, I had to gather my wits about me and figure out a way to get the sails down. They were causing some of the problem that was keeping us stuck. I felt the equatorial current running under the boat trying to push the boat to the west. I thought to myself, "If I could get the boat turned to starboard, maybe this current could actually help us."

I released the line to the mainsail, and the boom swung out over the port side of the boat. Every time another swell hit, the sail and the metal boom dipped into the water. I made my way forward to the main mast and released the main line that holds the sail up on the mast of the boat. She sat a bit more upright, and the impact of the swell lessened. I hauled in the boom and began to furl the Genoa, the forward-most sail. It came in easily. The boat sat even more upright.

As I started to furl in the Genoa sail, the bow lifted. The pressure being released from the sails and wind now allowed the bow to turn slightly to starboard. She was now sitting parallel to the two rows of rocks and bouncing on her keel. The equatorial current running through the reef did the rest. The boat slowly moved through one of the slots between the rocks. The next thing I knew, she was floating free. Thanks be to God!

> The boat slowly moved through one of the slots between the rocks.

I quickly checked for water below decks. None! The bilge monitor sat at three cycles, the same number as it had been that morning. I couldn't believe it. Maybe, just maybe, the boat would be saved. I called the coast guard and asked them to stand down, that the vessel was seaworthy enough to get back to our home port. I was grateful to hear them say they'd continue to monitor the situation. After hailing the coast guard, it was time to thank all the folks that were coming my way to our rescue. Tears streamed down my cheeks as I thanked each boat and captain.

As I checked to be sure there were no more rocks to hit, I saw the dingy about one hundred yards away. Paul had waited to see if I needed rescuing before taking the others to shore. I waved them over and welcomed them back on board.

I don't remember much of what I said or did after that. I was likely in some kind of shock. We turned the engine over, and she started right up (go figure). I watched the engine diagnostics very closely. The engine was intact, and we seemed to be running at the appropriate speed for the boat's RPMs, so maybe the propeller was good too. The thing that amazed me most was that the rudder was okay. The *Gypsy Wind* steered in both directions.

As we limped home, I kept checking that everyone was all right. They were fine. I was not. We laughed because they had never been at sea before, and what a story they had to tell their friends and neighbors back in Memphis! A local dive boat came up alongside to make sure we were okay. I gave thumbs-up to the captain. He smiled and went on to his dive site.

I was relieved and overjoyed that *Gypsy Wind* didn't become another Caribbean dive site, marked on one of the maps of sunken vessels. I imagined the note: *"Gypsy Wind*, a sixty-foot cutter ketch rig sailboat, dashed on Dry Rocks reef on a beautiful cloudless day in the Caribbean. She lies starboard side up, just to the west in sixty feet of water. The captain's poor judgment led to her demise. A large grouper occupies the captain's quarters. Some say there was treasure on board!"

As we headed into Lindbergh Bay, the steering quit. We poured a quart of hydraulic fluid into the steering box and went on our way. We later learned that the grounding had created a hydraulic leak in the steering mechanism located under my bunk, but *Gypsy Wind* had patiently waited until safe harbor before losing steerageway.

When we left our guests at the beach, I called to thank the coast guard and all the other boats that were listening for their help and prayers during our ordeal. Then totally exhausted, I crawled into my bunk and slept for two hours. When I awoke, I realized that I'd never be the same. My life had been changed forever.

It's hard to accurately describe the emotions I experienced that day on the water. Every time I think back on the entire episode, I notice that the same emotions are stirred within me, and I'm reminded of how all life is really a balance between smooth sailing one moment and then being slammed against the rocks the next.

I guess I learned three big lessons that day. First of all, never underestimate the power of a current running silently under your life.

Second, a number of small errors in judgment along the way can amount to a major problem down the road.

Third, when disaster strikes, do your damnedest to keep your wits about you.

I think that my ability to keep my focus, assess the situation quickly, and then execute a plan saved my boat and me. And it never hurts to have a little luck along the way.

Life lesson: Don't take shortcuts.

Life lesson: Most major problems begin with a series of minor problems.

Life lesson: Keep your wits about you when you are in a dangerous situation.

Life lesson: The same thinking that caused a problem cannot be used to solve it.

Repairs for Both of Us

The day after the accident, I sat and wept on the foredeck of *Gypsy Wind*. I'd let her down, putting her in harm's way and causing damage to her hull and the floor of the pilot house. It was such a strange feeling, like cheating on a girlfriend and getting caught. Intense shame and guilt filled every pore of my being. I had committed to care for and cherish her and then selfishly tried to shave a corner and take a short cut. She was hurt deeply. I sound like a total nut case, and maybe I am; but if I'd successfully navigated around the rocks and steered her safely to her anchorage, none of this would be happening. Duh!

> I'd lost my sense of competency as a good and capable boat captain.

Besides this, my pride was shattered. My sense of competency as a good and capable boat captain was as lost as a child that has wandered too far into the forest. It seemed as if everyone at the coffee stand every morning was staring at me like I was carrying a big sign that said, "This man wrecked his boat! He drove it up on the rocks! What a fool!" I was alone and lonely, lost and afraid.

Maybe it's posttraumatic stress from the accident. Whatever it is, it's like being disconnected from my body and looking at my pathetic self as others must see me. My closest friends say it's normal to go through this self-doubt and anxiety. My mind tells me to just get back at it again, but both my heart *and* my mate, Paul, say it's time to step back, assess the situation, and do the things that must be done to be sure we keep our future guests safe.

My friend and fellow boater, Steve Sullivan, came over today to look at the damage. He is a great guy from Rhode Island who is living his dream with his wife, Evelyn, and their very cool dog, Hanna (or Hanner, as Rhode Islanders say).

Steve said, "Thank God this boat was built in the seventies. Otherwise, you'd have big problems." He thought we should keep sailing her as long as she wasn't taking on water and then plan for repairs during her haul out next summer. We talked about an intermittent starting problem that we'd been having with Big Bertha, the Perkins one-hundred-twenty-horsepower engine that powers *Gypsy Wind*. Steve explained that we don't have a hot-engine-starting problem, but we have a "hot-cranking-engine-no-start" issue. I have no idea what he is talking about but vowed to find out.

I talked later that day to my then brother-in-law, Christopher Haun, on the subject. He explained that diesel engines need three things to run—fuel, compression, and air. That's it. If it doesn't start, it's one of those things. He's sure it's fuel-related. I felt much better after his no-nonsense chat and my subsequent lesson on diesel mechanics from my in-law.

So now it's time to heal my relationship with the boat. I vow to be more conscientious and stop taking unnecessary chances. I vow to be the caretaker she deserves and promise to apply all the lessons she teaches me.

So life goes on. Being a Monday afternoon, it's time to get cleaned up and take my "car," the seventeen-foot skiff, over to nearby Water Island for the weekly beach movies shown on a white sheet tied between two palm trees. "Only in the islands, Mon." This is the best example of island living I know of; motoring over to one of the most beautiful beaches on the planet at sunset with a rum drink in your hand, eating $2 cheeseburgers made by Heidi (the island version of Meals on Wheels), and watching old movies with friends and family. It doesn't get any better than this!

Except maybe not running the boat on the rocks in the first place.

Life lesson: When life changing events occur, take time to listen to what the event is telling you.

Boatspeak

The question is this: "What is the boat telling you? Is she happy?"

These were the words my mate said to me at dinner last night. I thought for a while and then agreed that they were the right questions, but I didn't know the answers. So I spent most of the night, as I have been doing recently, rolling back and forth in my bunk, asking questions, and listening for those answers.

The conclusion that no, the boat is not happy seemed so obvious. She was hurt and disturbed by the grounding last week, and I've been trying desperately to make everything appear all right. That is one of my MOs when I feel stressed about something. But the truth is, she is *not* okay. The boat has damage to her hull, the keel, and the rudder post. She has numerous interior cracks. The starboard fuel tank is out of position, the battery chargers are off their supports, and the hydraulic steering mechanism is leaking nasty, red automatic transmission fluid into the bilge. It looked as though the boat was bleeding. Everything is *not* all right, and continuing to pretend it is okay only hurts *Gypsy Wind* and me more each day.

> Everything is *not* all right, and continuing to pretend it is only hurts *Gypsy Wind* and me more.

The boat is telling me to pull her out of the water, get a hard look at the damage, and get her fixed. I need some time away from here and the boat. I want to see my kids and my family.

We made the decision that the Virgin Gorda boatyard would be the place to go. I so want this whole ordeal to be a non-ordeal. But it's big, and I needed to deal with it. After cancelling three charters, the call was made to the boatyard to arrange for a haul out for the boat and skiff. I'll give the rubber dinghy to my buddy Derek and keep the motor for a new dinghy in my future.

It occurred to me that my desire to do this work is fading fast. I'm losing confidence, more of it every day. I need some perspective to talk with someone who will be brutally honest. Kevin Maddock is the man to do this. He's a longtime boat captain here in the islands and picked me up from the airport my first night here. With his straightforward and honest style, I know he'll tell me his truth.

The boat needed to be repaired, to be happy again. I want her to sing again when she sails. Now her message is for people to stay away. She's becoming invisible to people on the beach. Maybe she's protecting them from what she knows could happen if we take them out on charter. Thank you, girl, for your wisdom.

So again I learn. *Gypsy Wind* speaks, and these are her lessons for me.

Don't put off doing what needs to be done just so you can save face and keep your fragile ego intact. Destroy your ego and all the false gods that keep it propped up. Open the doors to the Trojan horse and invite the enemy to emerge and be purged from your heart and guts.

Face the truth. Let it teach you. Don't try to cover up who you are. Once the veil of deception is removed, the beauty of your soul will emerge.

It's time to do some cleanup work. Stop pretending there's no water in your bilge. Do the dirty work. You will not be disappointed in the outcome. There will be no hidden damage. All will be out in the open where it belongs.

Get on with your calling. This is merely a short rest stop to refuel your internal engine and refocus on your calling. Get the internal damage fixed, so no part of you is a pretender anymore.

Get on with it.

Life lessons: Do what needs to be done no matter how it impacts your ego.

Night Wind

The following poem was written after the decision to haul *Gypsy Wind* out for repairs.

I finally slept through the night.
Decisions were made that caused my soul to rest.
The night wind blew effortlessly through the rigging
And I slept,

Without knowing, I knew in my heart of hearts
That to continue was not in her best interest.
I finally stopped and listened as she cried silently
And the night wind blew,

It was long after the pain went unnoticed that I woke up
from the dream that kept me from sleeping.
The nights had become so long and unbearable that I couldn't speak
Until the night wind blew into my cabin and spoke.

The night wind is the unseen character of grace
That moves softly across the water
And offers her help without intruding
Like a friend sitting in a dark room without speaking.

How can I ever repay her for being so patient
While I thrashed in my bunk through the painful night
And resisted turning my head so I could feel her touch on my face?
How can I ever thank her enough for waiting?

Then the night wind woke me from my misery, and I listened.
She said nothing, but I heard her speak through the cries of the chines
As they creaked and groaned with agony,
Wanting desperately for someone to listen.

After the night wind spoke, nothing.
Choices were made in the best interests of Gypsy Wind,
As my ego slowly melted into the sea
And I finally slept through the night.

Gypsy Wind in the boatyard on Virgin Gorda Island, British
Virgin Islands. Getting much needed repairs after the wreck.

Stopping the Carnival

A week after the accident, I finally woke up enough to go to sleep. It was in making the decisions I needed to make that I found relief from the internal torture I was putting myself through.

The boat needed to be hauled out of the water and all the damage fixed. I was resisting this thinking this would make me look incompetent as a captain and as a man. The damage to *Gypsy Wind* was the physical manifestation

> I wanted to believe that nothing really bad had happened to the boat, and I wanted to believe that nothing was wrong with me.

of what I was avoiding. I wanted to believe that nothing really bad had happened to the boat near Saba Island. And I wanted to believe that nothing was wrong with me internally. I wanted to pretend I was fine. Let the show go on. Don't stop the carnival!

And while I knew the truth all along, as we do most of the time, I pushed forward without paying attention to the obvious. That's been one of the underlying themes of my life—pushing ahead rather than stopping to evaluate the situation.

The key to finally sleeping was in the stopping and listening. The boat was crying for attention through her creaking and groaning. Before the day on the rocks, I never heard anything from her other than joyous laughter as her rigging sang in the breeze, and her sails snapped with glee as we tacked and jibed. Now she was in pain, and I was ignoring her. I wanted her to be okay, but in truth, I wanted *me* to be okay. But she wasn't fine any more than me. We were both hurt and needed a healing touch.

The following day, we sailed her to Virgin Gorda to the "hospital" at the Spanish Town boatyard. They will give her the love and the medical attention she needs. As for me, I'll travel back to Denver for two weeks to get the attention I need as well. I'll see my family and friends and finally sleep again.

You can't underestimate the power of decision making. After each decision to "do the right thing," I felt the weight of the pain lifting. I don't think I could

> After each decision to "do the right thing," the pain lifted.

have made any of these decisions until addressing some of my own internal needs. I needed the time—even if it was only ten days—to learn some life lessons from this misfortune.

And I learned this: Only when we gain perspective and let go of our notions about "what is best" can we learn and grow. I was hanging onto the irrational belief that I "had" to keep the boat in charter because this is the busiest month of the year. I believed that other people would belittle me if they saw my weaknesses and bad judgment. My ego was trying desperately to save face.

So many people actually live their lives just as I was, trying to keep up the good work and push forward. It's no wonder so many men have heart attacks in the "prime" of their careers. It may be due to their egos working overtime to "keep their ship in charter," so to speak. Just keep pushing forward. Don't pay attention to the obvious signs until the day you collapse on the kitchen floor holding your second cup of coffee.

When I'm on the water, I put my complete trust in *Gypsy Wind*. She is my home, my office, my recreation center, and my livelihood. The accident was my personal wake-up call when I was pretending all was well.

I've learned so many lessons through this experience that I could write for days. Maybe I will—after I get my second cup of coffee.

Life lesson: Sometimes it's best to stop our forward movement and stop and take stock of the present situation.

The Green Flash

The sailing season has come to an end for me this year. I'm both sad and relieved. I'm looking forward to being home again with friends and family, and it will feel good to dig in the garden and to plan where stuff will get planted.

Gypsy Wind will get good care this summer in Spanish Town, Virgin Gorda, one of the thirty something islands of the British Virgin Islands.

She will get the attention needed to repair the keel, rudder post, and portside cracks from the wreck. She'll get new bottom paint, new engine gauges and wiring, and new topside paint. They'll also finish sanding and refinishing the teak. Lots of work but plenty of time before the snow flies here in Colorado next November. Then late this fall, she'll be ready to go to work again.

She's still teaching me lessons from two thousand seven hundred miles away. That is astonishing to me. I look at her pictures like a young boy looks at his first love. I'm crazy about this boat. I find myself thinking of her at odd times of the day and night. I pause and imagine her lines and beauty as she glides through the waters of the Caribbean.

My favorite time on the boat is sunset. There's a ritual that I keep on the boat. Every day, no matter what the project, we stop ten minutes before sunset and sit on the deck, watching for the green flash—the rare atmospheric condition that causes a green spot right on the horizon at the moment of sunset. The last fraction of the sun to go over the horizon turns to an iridescent green! It doesn't happen often. The conditions must be just right for it to occur. I saw it just three times last sailing season. So there is an intrigue about it, both mystical and magical. I love watching for it, and I love seeing it. I miss it when I am not on the boat.

> I used to think everything had to happen *right now,* on *my* terms. But it doesn't. And it won't.

But life goes on. I've come to understand that waiting is a critical part of any process. I used to think everything had to happen *right now,* on *my* terms. But it doesn't. And it won't. Sitting quietly watching for the green flash after a busy day on the boat is one of the many activities I have adopted to help me slow down in life.

As I continue to agree more and more with what is, life gets easier and more enjoyable. Waiting all summer for *Gypsy Wind* to get repaired is painful, but at the same time, I'm learning about the process, trusting it, and letting it be.

This is a difficult thing for me to do. I like action all the time. I want it *now.* As I see it, this is part of the problem of our American culture. We've been trained by our cultural media to get things instantly.

Once my daughter and I were planning to stop at a fast-food joint to eat when I realized that I didn't have any money. I told her why we couldn't stop, and she said, "Why don't you just get some money from the money machine?" That was a profound moment. She actually thought that if you needed money, you simply went to a machine, and it gave you some. There was no connection for her that I might actually have to *earn* money before the machine would give some to me.

When I watch television, I'm amazed at how quickly any problem can be solved. In either thirty or sixty minutes, depending on the number of sponsors, any world crisis can be fixed! I get caught up in the same thinking. Why can't I get my garden to grow in just a couple of weeks? That's as insane as thinking that any of my own behavioral patterns could be changed or modified by simply saying so.

Any thinking pattern takes time to nudge out of its cozy little space in my brain. I may *say* I am changing, but it's the doing that makes it so. Putting into practice the changes I want to see in me is the key. It's like saying that I'm going to exercise. That's a nice thought, but until I get my ass off the couch, drag out my old bike, air up the tires, find my gloves and helmet, and head for the park, nothing changes! So often I agree to change or do something *with no intention whatsoever* of doing a damned thing. I say yes to something just to get it to go away! I also do this to change an uncomfortable subject, like saying, "Yes, honey, I'll call to schedule my colonoscopy." I say it, but I put it off as long as possible.

Admit it—you do too. Don't kid yourself into thinking you don't agree to things you will never do, at least not until someone nags you long enough. So get off your butt, get over to the phone, and make the call to schedule your colonoscopy (an interesting metaphor here).

I know . . . you'll do it just as soon as your show on TV is over. Right.

So whether I am lying in my hammock on the deck of the *Gypsy Wind* perseverating over all the bad stuff that could happen or sitting in traffic in downtown Denver tapping the steering wheel anxiously wanting the light to change on my terms, waiting is a part of life. The sooner I agree with the situation, the easier and more relaxed my life becomes.

And when it's time to take action, like changing course before the boat gets too close to the rocks or simply doing what I said I will do, the results are in the choices I choose to make. Consequently, I spend more time enjoying the moment versus getting more uptight.

Life lesson: Slow down and take time to enjoy the simple things like the sunsets, the gardens growing, the wind in the trees, and the clouds high in the sky.

Life lesson: Don't agree to do something you already know ahead of time you will not do.

Hoping for a Green Flash.

Part Three

The Other Side of the World

Home Yet Homesick

The *Gypsy Wind* is two thousand seven hundred miles away from me. On this Colorado morning, I sit and look at the just-budding daffodils and crocuses in the front yard. Light, high wispy clouds streak across the sky. It's beautiful, but feelings of sadness and discomfort stir within me while sitting by the warmth of the fireplace with my coffee.

The voice within my head keeps telling me, "You should be with the boat." It's like having a child in the hospital. You feel so helpless, and you long to be with them. I want to be with *Gypsy Wind*. Knowing that the guys on the island will take good care of her is comforting because there's really nothing I can do to fix her.

It's time to let go of the foolish notion of going back early. Staying focused on the present is hard, but it's what is needed now. Being with my son and daughter just as they each embark on a new path in the journey of their lives is a blessing. It's great being with them, but at the same time, it's somehow strained—they've already pulled away from me toward their own adventures. I feel removed from what each one is doing.

"Stay present," says the part of me that is often jumping ahead to what might be. I'm so very glad to be in the same place as my wife. She's an incredible supporter of my crazy dreams. She is an amazing partner for this chapter in my life. I'm grateful to her and to God for the connection we share.

So today, instead of wishing myself away from here, I'm getting stoked for one of my favorite activities—watching NASCAR racing on TV. I love to watch the cars go around in circles, forever turning left.

Tomorrow is soon enough to continue missing my *Gypsy Wind*. Today, it's beer and leftovers and watching the race with my son. We'll cheer on our favorite drivers and laugh and talk trash to each other all afternoon. What a great day!

Life lesson: When under stress, breathe, stay present, and deal with all the "shoulds" that are in your head.

Coy the Elder with Coy the Younger

Me on Planet Earth

Being back home in Colorado has given me an opportunity to sort through some of the bigger questions in life. There comes a time in every man's life when he must face some really big things. Stuff like, "Why I am here on the planet anyway?" or "What do I do with the rest of my life?"

A good friend, Jim Mitchell, once said to me, "Most men are born asleep, live their lives asleep, and die asleep." Author Paulo Coelho says he wants his epitaph to read, "He was alive when he died." That's a powerful statement!

Gypsy Wind has taught me that life is to be lived to the fullest, on the edge, and filled with the surprise and wonder of a child who finds his first arrowhead in the dirt. As we've spent the nights together, *Gypsy Wind* has taught me that my life is so insignificant yet so important.

When on the boat, I lie in the deck hammock, naming as many of the stars as possible from memory and guessing at the ones I'm learning. Then I stop and just stare into the dark space

> I just stare into the dark space between the stars. There is so much more dark than light.

between the stars. There is so much more dark than light. Then I imagine myself in a rocket ship, driving among the stars, speeding from one constellation to another in a matter of seconds. It's a glorious time!

Then the realization occurs to me that I'm in my hammock, on my boat, in Lindbergh Bay, on St. Thomas in the U.S. Virgin Islands in the Caribbean Sea, which connects to the Atlantic Ocean, in the northern hemisphere of Planet Earth, which sits in our solar system just far enough away from the sun that I don't freeze to death or turn into burnt toast if it was a little closer. And that sun and its planets sit on the outer edge of a massive group of stars called the Milky Way, which is just one tiny galaxy that I live in compared to many others. I feel really small when I go through that exercise. But it's not a *bad* small. It's a *grand* sense of smallness.

The smallness exercise helps me see that my problems are just as small. They may *seem* very big, but in the *really big* picture, they are microscopic. So I start to relax and see myself as a small but integral part of the universe. I am a player. Me. Getting to make up my life as I choose, every moment of every day, is one of the great revelations of my life. The moment my mind recalls this insight, my problems start to become more manageable

Life lesson: My problems are not near as large as I think they are in the grand scheme of life.
Life lesson: Life is made up of a huge number of choices we make. The better choices we make, the better life we have.

Dive Shop on Jost Van Dyke Island, BVI. Which way do we go?

How Far Can We Go?

The question we hear most often from the guests we take sailing is, "How far can we go?" They're asking a distance question—perfectly normal for people who lead linear lives. Most of our culture seems hell-bent on going farther than anyone before them.

This question is one that I asked myself before living aboard a boat. Now all the questions are different. Before *Gypsy Wind* came into my life, my tendency was toward a life that was linear as well. It's hard to get away from this kind of thinking when you're taught from a very young age that life is about *quantity*. How much can you do? How much wealth can you accumulate? How much *stuff* can you accumulate? How big can you get in the world? And all these questions are based on the belief that life is to be lived in a linear fashion.

People who choose to live under a different set of life parameters, if you will, are viewed by the masses as eccentric, weird, out-of-step, and confused. People who are more interested in deepening their understanding of themselves and the world are sometimes seen as misfits. You know, I sort of like the word *misfit*. I'm certainly becoming less "fitting" in the world than ever before.

> People who are more interested in deepening their understanding of themselves are sometimes seen as misfits.

I'm learning to slow down and see the world in a much different way than from what I was taught as a boy. My mother would tell me, "Books are for people who don't have anything better to do." And that resting and relaxing was not appreciated or condoned. If you took time for yourself, you were labeled as lazy. Life was about moving forward, finding a way to get past those who were ahead of you, using people to get the things that you needed so you could go faster and drive harder in the game of life.

I'm not sure when I started seeing the world differently from my parents (and for the most part, those around me), but I think it was about the same time I started a twelve-step program. My life had certainly been out of control for a while. I thought if I kept putting more wood on the fire, sooner or later I'd get where I was supposed to be.

But the older I got, the more I understood the idiocy of that proposition. It dawned on me that the only thing I was getting by living this was getting a bigger fire!

I looked at my coaching clients who were burning the candle at both ends and feverishly praying for more candles. They wanted me to help them stay in one piece as they hurled themselves through the atmosphere at breakneck speed. They were out of control, and so was I. I used various combinations of alcohol, sex, and prescription drugs to manage my own insanity.

And these worked for a time. I say "worked" in the sense that they kept me moving forward and on track to get whatever was waiting for me out there somewhere over the rainbow. How crazy is that?

In my recovery process, I encountered people who seemed to have stopped running the race of life. They'd stepped off the high-speed track and were really calm, genuine, and caring. I didn't perceive that they wanted something from me or that they wanted to use me in some manner. They just seemed to care about me with no ulterior motives. This was like a cool evening breeze that comes from the east after a long hot day on the water.

After starting my own recovery program, I realized how insane my life had become. Prior to my sailing life, I spent seventeen years as a counselor. Clearly, I had been a nut case—getting paid to listen to *other* nut cases and trying to help them get back on the racetrack again! This may be the major flaw in modern processes for the helping professions. We get paid (good money) to support the neurosis and insanity of our clients. That is *really* crazy.

In my executive coaching, I heard so many business leaders ask in different ways: "How can you help me get back in the game, to get back to my old self, to get back to making the big bucks?" These are all the wrong questions! The main reason these people had come to see me was because they couldn't keep up with the Joneses any longer. They had stumbled on the track and couldn't seem to get up, dust themselves off, and start again. My job was to help them get up, point them in the right direction, and send them on their way.

The following is an example of the insane manner in which we live our lives. One of my close friends was diagnosed with bleeding ulcers. After a week in the hospital, he went straight back to his office and continued where he'd left off. It was only a matter of weeks before he collapsed again. This time, he almost died. As he began to "wake up," he started to comprehend the treadmill he'd been running on for years. He has now stepped off the racetrack and says this: "Most men's lives are on autopilot, and they don't realize their altimeters are broken until they crash!" People are so consumed with what's next. They just want to know how far they can go.

> People are so consumed with what's next that they can't appreciate what's happening right now.

I'm not sure what's the best question to ask before going sailing, but it's not "how far can we go?" People need to think in terms of how much fun they're going to have or what they can learn from the wind and the sea. These questions produce an entirely different set of expectations. We could all use some of that medicine.

Life lesson: Slow down, breathe, and take time to smell the daffodils.
Life lesson: Start asking yourself better questions.

An Attack of the "Shoulds"

Today, I'm wondering when I'll be back in the water and offering charters once again. Will it be another week or another three weeks? I don't know, but there is calmness within me about the entire situation. Having done all that can be done it's time to wait. I'm better at this than I used to be.

Waiting is not at the top of my list of good qualities, but since figuring out why that's true, life has gotten a bit easier. I tend to be impatient and get edgy and irritable when forced to wait. Thinking about this, I finally understood: *forced* to wait. That was it! Who does the forcing in the waiting equation? It's me! What is that all about?

These feeling emerge whenever life doesn't follow my timetable, when something isn't happening at the rate of my own expectation. I could at last see that the "forcing" is done by me.

> The culprit in the equation—the self-imposed "shoulds"—that I place on myself and those around me.

When the guys at the boatyard *should* return my phone calls and e-mails and don't, I feel forced to wait. *There's* the culprit in the equation—the self-imposed "shoulds"—that I place on myself as well as those around me. The truth is, they simply haven't responded when I have decided they *should*.

In the same way . . .

The light *should* turn green sooner than it does. And that person in front of me *should* have turned in front of that oncoming car so I could turn when the light changed to yellow or even red. They *should* know that I'm in a hurry. The traffic *should* be clear in the middle of the day.

My children *should* act the way I want them to and do things how and when I want them to. They *should* be more considerate of my need for life to go faster.

My computer *should* never break down or run slower than I want it to run. It *should* maintain lightning speed all the time, no matter how slow the connection to the Internet. Everything on this earth *should* go at my pace—the correct speed.

You know, it's all "their" fault. I am blameless.

The construct we call time has become a demon for many of us. It grabs us and convinces us that we should be moving at X pace through the activity we call life. And when life doesn't jive with that internal pace clock, we get irritated.

As I'm learning, I'm more conscious about how people get irritated at life's pace. Look around at people who appear anxious and upset—often, it's the time thing. They desperately want life to move at the pace and time that they've predetermined, and it just doesn't. So they get upset.

I watch people who are constantly upset come to the islands to "relax" because the island pace is slower than wherever they came from. They want everything to happen on their terms. This seems most obvious to me in several places—the grocery store, in the car while driving, and at high-end resorts. They can't seem to adjust to a more relaxed pace while they are on the island.

One morning, I awoke on my boat to the sound of a man screaming at an attendant on the beach of the Ritz-Carlton. It was Sunday about 7:00 a.m., and he was ranting and raving about something. As you may know, sound carries on the water, so I heard the whole account. It was like having a front row seat at a WWF event!

He was from New York City and was explaining how important he was to the young beach attendant and that his morning would be completely ruined if he did not get his copy of the *New York Times* immediately. Even when told that the paper arrived on the airplane from New York later in the morning and he would get his paper then, that was not good enough. He screamed obscenities to anyone who would listen to his complaint.

I sat in the cockpit of my boat, sipping hot coffee, watching the entire drama unfold. Finally, one of the hotel managers was able to calm this poor soul by offering him a free night's lodging for his inconvenience.

I thought, "Wow! If I yell and scream enough, I'll be rewarded!" No wonder the man was out of his ever-loving mind. I think he knew that if he yelled long enough, he would get something from the resort. Amazing and completely insane.

He reminded me of one of my children when he was very young and wanted something he couldn't get. He pitched tantrums. In Arkansas, my home state, we call that a hissy fit. And for many months, we thought it easier to give in rather than experience the embarrassment of a three-year-old flopping around on the supermarket floor yelling at me that "it wasn't fair" that he couldn't have the candy he was craving. He had learned from our poor parenting that he should be rewarded for his actions. At his young age, he believed life should happen on his terms.

It amazes me how our beliefs control our emotions so much of the time. Our internal list of the way life "should" be sets us up for emotional meltdowns. The man from New York believed he should be able to get his paper when he wanted it, and my son believed he should get the candy he wanted. I believed that everyone in the boatyard should operate within my time frame. The "tyranny of the shoulds" is a powerful internal belief mechanism that can turn our everyday lives into pure hell

> The "tyranny of the "shoulds" is a powerful internal belief mechanism that can turn our everyday lives into pure hell.

If the island life has taught me anything, it's to slow down and take more time for everything in my life. And to realize that the barriers built for myself are just that—*what I build for myself*—thus creating the anxiety and frustrations that crop up in everyday life.

I am the director of my own play in the theater of life. The universe could care less about my being upset, mad, or whatever unpleasant emotion that is emerging in my life experience.

It was humbling and more than a little embarrassing to come to this stark realization, but it's made a big difference for me in terms of how my life is lived every day.

When you stop and think honestly about some of these "should," it's laughable! Some people never learn that sometimes the answer is "no" to our requests or even "not now but later." As I sat in amusement drinking my morning coffee, I realized that I'm grateful that I'm learning to wait. I see now that it builds character.

Oh, and I need to get a copy of the *New York Times* today.

Life lesson: Recognize that when we start telling ourselves when something "should" happen, we have slipped into thinking that the universe revolves around us.

I am.

I am weary.

I am weary of movement.

I am weary of movement of the boat.

I am weary. Of movement of the boat I am concerned.

I am weary of movement of the boat. I am more concerned when she sits.

I am weary of movement. Of the boat, I am more concerned when she sits still.

I am weary of movement of the boat. I am more concerned when she sits still in the boatyard.

"Soon Come," Safaris, and the Sea

My head is in the islands today, even though my body is sitting in Colorado. Thinking about the island lifestyle has me reflecting on a few things.

West Indians are delightful people with a pace of living that is so different from the typical American lifestyle. A good word to describe it would be *ambling*. West Indians aren't in a hurry about anything. I love it. Whenever something in the islands isn't happening as expected, the common response from a West Indian is, "Soon come."

This concept is best explained with a story about my buddy, Glenn McBrearty. He was waiting for a ferry ride from one island to another. It didn't show up when it was scheduled, so he sat patiently for a while. Then he began to wonder when or even *if* the ferry was coming. He finally approached the toll booth and asked about it. The attendant said he didn't know when the ferry would arrive. "Well," Glenn said, "can you give me some idea?" The response was "soon come." When Glenn pushed a little more, the man said he meant that the ferry might "soon come today, maybe tomorrow."

This is a wonderful example of island living. It's not that people don't care. It's that they truly *don't know* when an event will take place or *if* it will take place at all. They are being totally honest in their response.

> West Indians seem to think that an automobile is simply something to get you from one conversation to the next.

Here's another example of the pace of the islands. West Indians seem to think that an automobile is simply something to get you from one conversation to the next. Locals make tourists (those who dare to drive on the left side of the road) crazy by stopping in the middle of busy streets to chat with friends. They also stop anywhere to allow other drivers to enter a street or roadway in front of them. It's cheap and great entertainment watching tourists go bananas at the island driving style.

The best way to do this is to ride a safari bus across the islands. Safaris, or "the dollar ride" as locals call them, are open-air taxis that carry on average fifteen people. I can ride all the way around the east end of St. Thomas for only $3! And the rides are always very refreshing and relaxing. A safari ride gives me a chance to interact with the local culture in an enjoyable way.

Every ride is not pleasant though. One day a woman who obviously had some emotional issues boarded the bus and began screaming at everyone that we passed. Now and then, a rider will have had too much rum before boarding, and they snore as you're riding along beside them through paradise. It's great fun!

I've also learned to find joy in the most natural things. I've never felt more alive than when we're sailing across the blue Caribbean waters. The smells, sights, and sounds are hypnotic. I never want a day or a sail to end. As *Gypsy Wind* glides through the swells, it feels heavenly, like floating along on a cloud of turquoise. It's surreal at times.

> I've never felt more alive than when we're sailing across the blue Caribbean waters. I never want a day or a sail to end.

One day, along the north shore of St. John Island, we spotted two dolphins. They made their way to our bow wake, and we saw a newborn between them. The parents were teaching the baby to ride the bow wake of my boat! It was one of the most beautiful things I've ever seen. Their grace and playfulness reminded me how we ought to live.

On other charters, we've seen humpback or pilot whales; and almost every day, we spot at least one green sea turtle. When my sister came to visit last winter, she and her husband swam with a very large sea turtle. The look on her face when she returned to the boat was priceless! She couldn't believe how close she had come to a truly wild animal.

The island life has a way of teaching me to be grateful for the simplest things. The first time I said "soon come" to someone who was frustrated that a bus was late, he looked at me as if I were crazy. Maybe I am. But I don't think I will be getting ulcers any time soon.

Life lesson: Take time to appreciate the simple things in life.

Where Do I Go from Here?

I've been away from my boat for too long. She is calling me. The repairs should be done within the next three weeks, and I want to be there when she's ready.

In the meantime, life has been interesting. As I get quiet, I find myself filled with uncertainty about what lies ahead for *Gypsy Wind* and me. I need to hear from her—and from my heart—about what's next in life for me. More and more, the realization is occurring that we may not be able to earn enough doing charters, but that could change next season if we can stay in Lindbergh Bay. Time will tell.

Thoughts turn to getting someone to run the charter business for me and live and work on the boat. That would free me to pursue this writing notion that burns within, and it would allow more time to teach and mentor younger sailors—two things I love.

Getting a sense of what our purpose is on the planet is not as easy as deciding which car to buy. But at the same time, I'm seeing that we start to gain a feeling for what is right for us when we slow down and find ways to start listening to the longings of our hearts. I believe we can know our calling by slowing down, taking stock and discovering our deepest desires. The mystery is not in finding our purpose but rather figuring out how to live it on a daily basis.

> The mystery is not in finding our purpose but rather figuring out how to live it on a daily basis.

From my observations, most people seem to simply follow whatever is next. They just do the next thing that life throws at them. I call this "default living." I've certainly spent enough time myself living that way. But it's possible to learn to live our lives more intentionally—with purpose.

While slowing down long enough to begin the listening process, I discovered a number of interesting things. One is a desperate desire to be creative. Having some sort of project going at all times allows my creative juices to flow. Without this, my happiness and fulfillment factors go *way* down. I also discovered a deep desire to help men learn to wake up and live their lives with more passion, presence, and purpose.

Constantly being on the lookout for opportunities to practice these two desires has created more enjoyment in life. Before I understood what I really wanted, just heading for whatever looked like greener pastures was my *modus operandi*. It's been said, "Most people don't know what they want in this life, but they are pretty sure they don't have it." This statement puts it in a nutshell.

Life lesson: Learn to lean into and live your purpose on planet earth.
Life lesson: Figure out what you really want in life and go after it.

Almost ready to splash and get back to work.

Thanks, Teddy

A dear friend learned about my mishap with *Gypsy Wind* on the rocks west of St. Thomas and sent me this poem. I wept when I read it. Doubting my skills and abilities as a boat captain, the thought of never sailing again was grinding away within me like the coral reef that ground against the keel of my boat. I will forever be indebted to my good buddy, Tim Lane. This poem gave me the courage to hold my head up, keep moving forward, and continue to pursue my dream.

The credit belongs to the man who is actually in the arena,
whose face is marred by dust and sweat and blood,
who strives valiantly,
who errs and comes short again and again,
who knows the great enthusiasms, the great devotions,
and spends himself in a worthy cause;
who at best, knows the triumph of high achievement;
and who at the worst, if he fails,
at least fails while daring greatly,
so that his place shall never be with those cold and timid souls
who know neither victory nor defeat.

— Theodore Roosevelt
Citizen in a Republic, April 23, 1910

Dinner with friends. Warren Smith, Capt Coy, Tom Bryant, and Big John

My "back yard" in front of the Ritz Carlton Resort on St Thomas, USVI

Cocktail Hour with Dear Friend Capt Jordan Barrow
after a hard days work on the Gypsy Wind

Repairs complete and new paint job. Launching day.

Finally back in the water!!

Fore deck looking aft

Cooking lunch for guests aboard the Gypsy Wind.

Snorkeling at Grass Cay between Tortola, BVI and Jost Van Dyke, BVI.

Pirate's Week at the Ritz Carlton. We buried
treasure on the beach for kids to find.

Sailing with guests east of Red Hook, St Thomas, USVI

A fine day at the office.

Part Four

Back in the Islands

Taking Advantage of a Delay

Returning to the Islands to get a firsthand look at the work on the boat was imperative. It just so happened I had scheduled a term charter for three days, so I took advantage of coming to Virgin Gorda to see my boat in the "hospital." Today I got my first up-close look at the work being done on *Gypsy Wind*. The exterior repairs were almost complete, but actually getting into the boat was a different story. More than a week ago, I e-mailed the boatyard to leave her unlocked so I could stay there and do some little repairs myself. "No problem, Mon" was the response from the boatyard superintendent.

But when I arrived midday on Saturday, the boat was locked. No one from the boatyard was around to help. Perfect! I'd come two thousand seven hundred miles to check on my boat and couldn't get in. There were a couple of choices. Breaking a window was one, or prying off the lock and breaking the wood around it was another. But looking at her and realizing that this is an island thing helped me calm down. After stewing for a few minutes, I walked back to the dock and caught the next island-hopping ferry back to St. Thomas.

> Blue skies and turquoise water! What more could an old salt ask for?

The only redeeming part of this trip was a chance to go sailing. I had a term charter with a couple from Denver, and we spent three days basically motor sailing because the wind was too light. But the weather was awesome. Blue skies and turquoise water! What more could an old salt ask for? Well, maybe some wind, but we had a great time despite the lack of breeze. The clients left happy, and that's all that really mattered to me.

On my way back to St. Thomas for the third time on this trip, some wonderful souls at the ferry terminal at the West End of Tortola struck up a conversation. We chatted over cold Heineken beer while waiting for our ferries to arrive. They mentioned that they were heading over to a nearby island, Jost Van Dyke, for a few days. They had lots of questions about what they should see and do while they were there.

It occurred to me that my plane out of St. Thomas didn't depart for another twenty-four hours, so I invited myself along as their personal tour guide for the evening and next morning and proceeded to purchase a fare to join them.

That evening, my new best island friends were introduced to Vinny and Debbie, the owners of Corsairs Restaurant, for a grand meal of calamari ceviche salad and conch fritters, followed by roasted chicken with white wine sauce. After a couple of their famous "painkillers," my new friends started feeling like they were becoming locals. We ended our evening dancing in the sand at the world famous Foxy's Island Bar as a live band played songs from the Island's legendary Bob Marley and the Wailers.

The next morning, I found myself sitting at Ivan's Stress-Free Bar on Jost Van Dyke, overlooking White Bay with the Caribbean Sea beyond and drinking coffee, a perfect place to start any day. After stopping to say good-bye to my buddies at the restaurant and vowing to get together when they came to Denver later in the summer, I headed to the ferry dock.

My travels took me back to St. Thomas to meet some friends before heading home to Colorado for the summer season. I'll miss this beautiful place but plan on returning next fall with high hopes for a good season. If only I can get the keys to the boat by then.

Life Lesson: Take time to drive down the backroads of life.

The Life I Choose

As the summer slowly gave way to fall, I realized it was time to head south back to the life I had chosen. The repairs on *Gypsy Wind* were almost complete, and there was a long "laundry list "of stuff the needed attention. The anxiety within me on the first night back in the islands was higher than a teenager on a first date. Fitful sleep was broken by a terrifying nightmare. I was dying in some way, swirling around in a vortex, being pulled beneath blue-black waters.

After the dream, something shifted. With a loose foothold of understanding, I saw that nightmares, day sweats, and panic attacks were the side orders of the PTSD that followed the main dish of terror after crashing my boat the previous sailing season. But we survived the ordeal; I saved my boat, and most important, nobody got hurt.

At least until this week. Unknowingly, this sailor was severely traumatized by that experience. A fear of people crept over me like fog around the Golden Gate Bridge. Crowds stirred panic attacks deep within my soul. I was a mess, a self-diagnosed train wreck. But understanding what was happening (with the help of friends), I started to get a grip. I needed my boat. I needed to sit on my boat, to hug my boat, and to cry on my boat. I had to leave the fast pace of St. Thomas and find a quiet place and some measure of peace.

> I know I was severely traumatized. I felt paralyzed. I was a mess, a self-diagnosed train wreck.

After landing back on my island home of St. Thomas, I took the ferry to Virgin Gorda Island where my boat sat on the dry ground. When we arrived at the dock, a woman greeted me with a big smile. It was my friend Irene from St. Thomas coming to meet her husband, Al, who had crewed on a boat race down from the States. In fact, it was the annual Caribbean 1500. There were boats, people, calypso music, and food everywhere. But it felt different from the craziness of the bigger island.

A warm easterly breeze was blowing. People were laughing and telling sea stories of their long offshore adventures. I felt right at home. I also felt welcomed by Al and the other crew members who had been sailing on a beautiful boat named *Nepenthe* with Captain John. We drank and laughed and ate until late into the night.

Gypsy Wind was waiting patiently for me to return and take her back to the sea. Running my hand across the sleek lines of her hard underbelly and along her keel helped me reconnect with my boat and my dream. I was glad to be home with my boat. Our lives had become intertwined as she had saved my life, and her demise had been spared. Seeing the repairs at the boatyard brought a huge smile to my face, and tears of joy fell from my eyes. With a fresh paint job, she looked beautiful, even in the harsh streetlight that cast long shadows across the boat yard.

But she was dirty after being in the yard for six months, and first light tomorrow would bring a much needed washing. Starting a cleaning job on the outside of the boat might be a bit counterintuitive, but it makes me feel good to see a sterling clean sailing vessel in the yard.

The sunrise woke me, and with coffee in hand, the boat washing commenced. When that was done, I sat on the deck and started making a list on a crumpled piece of paper from my pocket. This paper would become completely shredded by the time all the chores were checked off the long list of "stuff" that needed to be done before she was to go back into the water. The order of cleaning would emerge based on cost, time, difficulty, and what we referred to as "the pain-in-the-ass factor." The latter often took precedence over the others, especially toward the end of a long, hot day.

But hard work in the islands starts to slow as the sun begins reaching for the horizon. Even the music in the boatyard begins to morph toward reggae and calypso. Everyone begins to unwind by sitting on his or her boat decks high above the ground. Strangers begin conversations about what they did or didn't get done today by offering a cold beer to a fellow boater.

One of the beautiful things about the work ethic in the islands is that West Indians are not driven so much by the almighty dollar. They stop working at a reasonable time so they can spend their evenings with family and friends. It's a good way to live. This is the life I choose.

But on a blazing hot afternoon during one of the many hours of teak work, it dawned on me that I couldn't do this. It was not the work or the heat but rather a deep gnawing feeling like you get before final exams when you haven't opened the textbook all semester. Thinking about launching the boat, sailing her back to St. Thomas, and facing the Ritz-Carlton crowd seemed totally impossible to me.

In the past years, as every day in the boatyard was over, my excitement level grew with the anticipation of seeing my boat being lowered by the crane into the blue Caribbean water. There was nothing more satisfying than the act of putting a line through each task on my tattered paper list that brought me closer to sailing again.

But this year, it was as if a great undertow of dread and doubt was holding me in its grasp. I was frozen and could not accomplish all the tasks that needed to be done to get the boat in the water. I was severely depressed and needed help now.

Life lesson: Make a list of everything that needs to be done and then check them off when each is done.

Life lesson: Pay attention to your inward state of being. If you need help, get it.

Chickens in the Trees

Geoff and Chris comprise a father-son team who run the repair services in the boatyard on Virgin Gorda. They're delightful Englishmen, kind and soft-spoken. They make me feel good. We're going to work together to get things done right.

The boat is coming back to life once again. She's getting a fresh coat of bottom paint now. All the scars from the wreck are gone from the boat but not from my heart and psyche. I'm still feeling fragile emotionally. Today, I'm going to start staining the teak. Although it will take a few days, time is on my side at this point.

But with every stroke of the paintbrush, the feeling of dread moves more and more into the forefront of my mind. My depression is growing by the day. It's only a small respite to get out of the boatyard for a night.

Last night was my buddy Ed's birthday. He and his beautiful wife, Tina, are friends from St. Thomas. They live in Vermont in the summers and, down here in the winters, on their Beneteau sailboat, *Chico*, a very efficient boat with the feel of home inside. Very cozy.

Last night, we celebrated Ed's birthday at the Mine Shaft Restaurant. We drank their signature drink—the Cave-In. One was enough to bring me to my knees. Then we enjoyed a feast of ribs, chicken, and all the fixings. The coleslaw reminded me of some that I've had in Arkansas.

The view from the restaurant was stunning. It's the highest point on the west end of Virgin Gorda Island, with a view to the west all the way to St. Thomas. Incredible! Perhaps the best part of our evening was a tree in front of the restaurant that was full of chickens! Apparently, they roost in the treetops at night to avoid predators. Seeing a Rhode Island Red rooster perched on a frangipani tree at dusk was the highlight of my night. Only in the islands!

I'm losing weight on a "one meal a day" plan. It saves money and gets me out of the boatyard at night to talk with people. So far, so good! But I can feel a storm brewing somewhere deep in my psyche. I have to get out of here sooner rather than later. After informing my friends in the yard that I am leaving for a while, the ferry dock is my next stop. I tell Keith Thomas, the yard manager, to cancel the boat launch that was scheduled for later in the week.

I feel as though I am drowning in despair, and there is no one in sight to help me as the rip current of doubt draws me under again and again. And Thanksgiving weekend is approaching, and there is no place for me to go for dinner. I am feeling as if I am the only person in the islands with no friends and no place to go. I am adrift in a sea of emotion.

After boarding the ferry and heading west down the Sir Francis Drake channel, I look back at my boat with tears filling my eyes. Upon my arrival on St. Thomas, I drift past the coffee stand to say hello to my friends Karen and Mike, owners of the coffee stand aptly named *Lattes in Paradise*. I must have looked forlorn because they invite me to sleep on their couch and join their family and friends for Thanksgiving dinner. They will never know how much their offering helped me start healing. I am filled with gratitude.

Life lesson: Take stock of your emotional state on a regular basis.

A Little Help from My Friends, Part 1

After a week on Mike and Karen's couch, I've taken refuge on Water Island. It's one of the smaller islands in the USVI, and it's been a lifesaver on several levels for me.

A few days ago, I was still locked up with intense fear and anxiety that left me cloistered in the living room of their home, wondering if my life was worth living. I was really scared. I can't remember the last time I'd felt so despairing and hopeless.

> It had been quite a while since I last visited the soul of me.

After several attempts on my own (the key phrase here is "on my own") to unsuccessfully shake this emotional weight from my shoulders, I contacted Kevin. I will always be grateful that he was willing to meet me for lunch the following day.

When we met, I babbled about experiencing what recovering therapists labeled as post-traumatic stress disorder because of the flashbacks about the accident. Kevin listened patiently and then said bluntly, "I don't know much about this PTSD or whatever you call it, but I have lots of experience with fear."

Noticing over lunch that I was feeling extremely fragile when I arrived back on St. Thomas, my friend (and mentor) Kevin and wife Cindy have graciously given me some time in their home on Water Island. He's been a recovering alcoholic for many years and has much wisdom to offer. Cindy offers her unconditional love and compassion to my healing. My friend Glenn calls this oasis "Camp Kevin." For me, it was a spiritual retreat. I received much needed healing by spending time with Kevin and Cindy as well as with myself. It had been quite a while since I last visited the soul of me.

As he spoke, the still small voice within me knew that he was the right person to be talking with just then. Kevin is no-nonsense, hard-nosed, matter-of-fact, and filled with compassion for people who want help. My kind of guy.

So we began a process by cataloging everything I was afraid of or made me anxious. I ended up with over seventy fears about people, things, and what I call "stuff"—all the roadblocks in life that cause fear and anxiety to emerge.

Then I considered how those fears affected me—my self-esteem, my pocketbook, my personal relationships, my ambitions, and a number of other things. Realizing how much I was afraid of, I thought, "No wonder I'm an emotional mess right now!"

The next step was observing my behavior when feeling fearful. It didn't take long to realize that I was a selfish, dishonest, self-seeking, self-reliant person who was attempting to live life using coping skills I'd learned during my formative years. Now many years later, I was using skills that "got me through" during my self-diagnosed crazy years. Thinking about all these survival skills, it dawned on me that they were not working any longer.

When I'd identified and accepted all that, the puzzle pieces of my life started to come together. I was using all the self-esteem builders that had failed me once before, and by God, they were failing me once again! Isn't it interesting that we can so easily trick ourselves into believing that we have our proverbial act together? I was living on borrowed time, and my clock was running out. I was on the verge of completely crumbling into some sort of babbling idiot, with a belly full of rum to boot.

Now on this island, after a few days of clarity, I see that my head was totally filled with things that kept me from seeing myself honestly. I'm starting to get a new picture today. At this moment, some internal mending is taking place. I still have to go back out into the real world and face everything that was there when I left last week. And I *will* go out, with the grace of God, and make a go of it with all that I've got. I'm reminded of a quote on a leadership-class poster I'd taught: "I must do it myself, and I can't do it alone."

I'll give it my best effort, and if, for whatever reason, that's not enough, I'll go home with my head high and, with humility, accept whatever fate holds for me and my career. I'll be able to say that it was a great ride and that the lessons learned during this grand adventure will serve me well, however I end up.

But for now, the thought of failure is out of my mind. Trusting my higher power to guide me through all this mess is at the forefront of my thinking. So tomorrow, I'll return to *Gypsy Wind* and work diligently on her teak and prepare her for another season of service here in the Virgin Islands. And I'll work on myself too.

Life lesson: When you need help, ask for it!
Life lesson: Recognize when you are using old ways of coping that are no longer working for you and develop healthier ones.

A Little Help from My Friends, Part 2

The mentoring and support from Kevin had a profound impact on me. At the same time, something else was also mentoring and teaching me. It was a coconut. While I have been here at Kevin and Cindy's, I've gone down to the beach most days. Quiet little Spratt Bay on the southeast corner of the island is one of the most beautiful places on earth, with its half-moon shore lined with coconut palms. Some of them reach out over the edge of the water, and others sway in the background. The beach is covered with small shells, and the turquoise Caribbean water gently laps at my feet as I look south where you can see St. Croix Island on clear days. When I stand there, it feels like a B-movie set, and soon some ravishing woman in a skimpy bikini will come sauntering out of the trees. It's magical, to say the least.

So today, I headed down to this beach after a day of staring at it from Kevin's front deck. No one else was down there. This entire paradise is mine today. I sit, read, swim, snorkel, and walk the beach, looking for stuff and watching. It's the watching that I must tell you about.

> It was a coconut rolling back and forth on the beach. I think this image may have changed my life forever.

The first day of my time here, I went to Spratt Bay late in the afternoon, and the colors and light were turning in the bay into a photographer's dream. I chose a spot out of the sun to sit and ponder my life. After about twenty minutes, I suddenly "saw" what I had been casually staring at. It was a coconut rolling back and forth on the beach. The water pushed it up the slight beach incline, and then it rolled back down on its own. This image may have changed my life forever.

It occurred to me that maybe somehow—God, the Universe, Spirit, or whatever—was trying to tell me something. I kept watching the coconut as the water pushed it up the beach, and it rolled back, time and time and time again.

I sat for a while longer, simply watching. The more I watched, the more I began to see. All at once, I began to relate to this coconut. *I am not kidding.* I got up and walked over to it for a closer look at what was happening. Everything about my life was right there. Everything.

I began to imagine what it would be like to have no control over your life at all, to simply *be* there and wait until the next wave pushed you around. The more I studied this coconut, the more I began to see what the universe was offering me. This was my life—I was allowing fear to push me around. I was at the mercy of whatever the next fear would be.

Then things started to get *really* weird. I thought how this coconut must have fallen from one of the trees that reached out over the water. This poor coconut had probably spent all his time pondering what he would do with his life if he ever had the chance to fall from the tree. I imagined him looking out and seeing St. Croix on the horizon and wishing he could go there. He had seen many boats come and go from the bay over the years, so he knew there was life beyond this spot.

Then I thought about how he must have felt when he finally fell to the sand. He was stuck where he was until the moon was full and the high tide invited him on a great journey! But then things went wrong. He couldn't get off the beach! No matter what he did, he was just stuck there, all alone, being pushed back every time he tried to make a run for it. (By the way, I was not under the influence of any mind-altering substances during any of this adventure with Mother Nature. I was morbidly sober and relatively lucid.)

I kept watching. Occasionally, the coconut would make it past the first set of waves, and he'd bob up and down ecstatically like he was thrilled to be off the beach. But just moments later, he'd get picked up by a bigger wave and was tossed up on the beach again.

And I thought, "This is me. I'm on the beach of possibility, and the damned waves of fear are keeping me pinned here!" Feeling completely powerless to do anything, I would just have to wait and hope for something or someone to get me out of my predicament. I was miserable and getting confused watching my coconut friend rolling around on the sand. Textbook victim role! Woe is me.

Finally, I simply wished my new friend good luck and headed back to the house filled with insights—and a few thoughts that bordered on the insane.

The following day, I decided to do a little snorkeling. As I rounded the corner to walk down to the water, guess who was there? My buddy! He'd waited there for me all night. And he was doing the same exact thing—rolling up and down the beach, as the waves of fear controlled his destiny.

It was wonderful being back in the water again. It felt good to swim to the mouth of the bay and watch all the fish and sea creatures that I've come to see as friends after spending time taking people on sailing and snorkeling tours.

And when I returned to the beach, there was Coco. By this time, I had to name him, and this one seemed to fit. He also seemed to like it. As I watched Coco do his thing, I wondered if he would ever break free from the waves that held him.

I wondered the same thing about myself. Some of my own waves of fear began way, way back.

Then I realized that Coco was actually making some progress! He was a little farther down the beach than he was yesterday. I did some quick calculations and figured that he must have been at this for about four days. That's a lot of rolling back and forth. Looking closer, I saw that the sand had scrubbed off his outer layer of green skin, exposing what looked like red hair. When he bobbed in the water, his hair hung down. It was like something from the sixties, and it looked great on him! He was a long-haired wanderer out to make a break from his boring life on the beach.

I expected that to be my last encounter with Coco. It was not. Returning on the third day, I saw that he was continuing his journey. He was making his getaway. He had finally worked his way to a place on the beach where the waves had less impact on him. I fully expected him to make his break in the next day or so. And I knew I would too.

He had found an inner strength that allowed him to harness the waves and reach his own resources.

On my last trip to the beach, I found Coco resting on the rocks that lined the western edge of this beautiful place. He had somehow managed to reach an even higher position, and the waves no longer had him in their grip. He seemed at peace, just lying there being a coconut. He had made a long journey down the beach and had found a new resting place. Coco is my hero. He fought the waves of fear and managed to get past his former place in life to come to rest in a protected corner of Spratt Bay.

Coco has been a great inspiration to me. At first, I pitied his plight. But after watching him tenaciously tackle the waves every day and still find a way to break free, I saw how he used his fear to help him ultimately get off the beach. Once he had been at the mercy of those waves, but he found an inner strength that allowed him to harness their power and reach his own resources.

This coconut has made a huge impact on my life. He has been a teacher and a friend in some strange, esoteric manner. (You may be wondering why I didn't I help Coco by throwing him farther out beyond the waves to make things a little easier for him. I thought about it, but it just didn't seem the right thing to do. He had his life, just as I had mine.)

Perhaps he even drew some sort of hope from *me*. I'd like to think he did. But I left Coco right where life had put him, believing he was at peace.

I did, however, take a very small coconut with me when I left the beach for the last time. He was empty, his insides destroyed by some force of nature. I've given young Coco Jr. a place of honor on my boat. He reminds me that if you don't get yourself to the water and face your waves of fear, you could be devoured from the inside by something else.

Armed with a fresh approach to my life, I am ready to get back to *Gypsy Wind*, get her ready for the new season, and start sailing once again.

Life lesson: Lean into your fear and use it to free you from its grip and
   control.
Life lesson: Take time to allow nature to teach you lessons that you
   need to learn.

No Regrets

I wake from a deep slumber to a squall with hard-driving rain and gusts of wind in the high twenty-knot category. I'm dry and secure in the captain's quarters of the *Gypsy Wind*. She sits stately in the early morning hours with her bow pointed into the wind, accepting all that nature offers her. She is a magnificent sailing vessel. Her life is being restored, and I am the beneficiary of her grace. We are a gift to each other.

> Deep within me, there is a stirring, wondering if *Gypsy Wind* has been teaching me more than I really care to learn at this point in my life.

In a couple of hours, we'll ready the boat for the guests who will be on board with us today. By then, the weather may have changed drastically into a pristine Caribbean morning. But until then, I have time to think. As I ponder the past years, I'm slowly coming to see that I really *am* as crazy as some of those around me believe me to be. I've undertaken the monumental task of starting a sailing business in a foreign country, as well as resurrecting a rundown sailboat after she'd sat rotting in the boatyard for a number of years. Either of those might put someone in the crazy category.

Most of *Gypsy Wind*'s systems work well, not withstanding an occasional glitch. The major work was in the cosmetic area. She has plenty of teak that gives her much of her charm. But with teak comes endless hours of work. Every square inch of the wood on the boat needed to be sanded down to bare wood and then two coats of stain applied, followed by at least three coats of marine gloss finish. It was an exhausting task.

Deep within me, there is a stirring, wondering if *Gypsy Wind* has been teaching me more than I really care to learn at this point in my life. I could be sitting at home in a cozy office with a nice little consulting practice, telling people how they could better run their business, perhaps doing some personal coaching, helping folks to get clear about what they want in life.

It's been said that most people don't know what they want in life, but they're pretty sure they don't have it. After jumping full force into a new business and a pirate ship restoration project and realizing my dream and getting what I wanted, I'm starting to wonder if it's what I want now. And that's a different dilemma altogether.

I vacillate between pure pleasure and misery. My nights are spent wondering what in God's name have I gotten myself into with this project. Most of my days are filled with angst, wondering if any guests from the resort will sign up to go sailing today.

But on this splendid morning, after the clouds departed and the wind and seas calmed, I sat on *Gypsy Wind*'s foredeck at sunrise, sipping strong black coffee, listening to the birds singing, thinking this may be the most challenging project (after parenting) that I've ever undertaken. But hey, it's just life, and I got what I wanted.

With all dreams come a few nightmares. But I've dared to dream. By casting off the lines of security and comfort and pulling up the anchor of predictability to reach a vision held in my heart for almost forty years, I am what I dreamed of becoming—*a sailboat captain with his own charter business*. And after taking the risks and stepping out on pure faith, I will not look back and say to myself, "You never should have done that." And when my days on earth are almost over, may it be said with all honesty to those around me, "I have no regrets."

Life lesson: With every dream, there are nightmares along the way.
Life lesson: Dare to dream. For without dreams, we are merely spectators
   in the game of life.

Counting My Blessings

The journey continues. I'm on the *Gypsy Wind* writing. It's rained constantly since last night. The sun peeked through the gray clouds for the first time today at 3:50 p.m. That's unheard of in the islands. But there was a good side to this. I got some reading done and fixed a freshwater problem we've had for about a month. Then my body and soul enjoyed a half-hour swim and a much-needed and appreciated "God shower" on the deck in the pouring rain. It was very enjoyable, to say the least, after taking saltwater showers for the last week.

> The boat continues to teach me life lessons. Every day I learn something about myself

When you're living on a boat, everything takes more time. My world is constantly moving back and forth and up and down. And I love it more than I can say. The boat continues to teach me life lessons. Every day I learn something about myself. Today's lesson is to be more grateful and appreciative of all the little things in the world, like sunshine and warm breezes and even rain—the boat is cleaner than she's been in a month.

Here is my current list of all the things I am thankful for:

Comfortable beds
Free Internet
Limes
Rum
Friends, old and new
Skimpy bikinis
Clean sheets
Skype
An engine that starts every time
Warm rain

Good burritos
Did I mention friends?
Spotted eagle rays
Great coffee

Today *does* feel like the first day of the rest of my life. And I can't wait to live it to the fullest of my abilities.

The charter business has been slow to start this season, but I'm learning to be patient about things beyond my control. I'm spending most of my time on a never-ending to-do list of boat projects. There are many lessons about electricity these days and how batteries work (or don't) in the tropics. I must force myself to tackle some of these projects because of the lethargy that comes with living on the water.

It amazes me how lazy people become after they move to the tropics. I can't be sure if they were that way before they moved down here or became that way afterward. It puzzles me when people are continually coming up with all the reasons for their inactivity. And here, I am becoming just like them.

Actually, it's very easy to get into the "mañana mentality." The heat, the salt, and the warm sea breeze all contribute to a lazy lifestyle. To be honest, there are times when the urge to put off until tomorrow what could easily be done today must be fought vigorously. But when I do get up and get something done that day, I always feel better about myself and my circumstances.

My first mate Derek is not one that has been infected with a case of becoming lazy. He is a great catch in a sea of slackers. Thank God he is on the boat this season as he keeps me moving forward on the days when I would rather just say *mañana*.

Life lesson: Find someone that can encourage and support you when you are feeling down and out or just lazy.
Life lesson: An attitude of gratitude is the key to happiness.

A Story from My First Mate

Derek Kellenbeck was the last first mate on *Gypsy Wind*. I asked him to write a story about one of his personal experiences on the boat. This is his story.

One of my most memorable experiences on the *Gypsy Wind* was the night we rode out a tropical storm that blew through in early December. In the early evening, we started preparing the *Gypsy Wind* for what we thought would be some mild wind and a little ocean swell.

For good measure, we decided to put down a second anchor just in case things really started bucking. As we attempted to run out the second smaller anchor, we realized there was a glitch in that anchor system. No matter what we tried to do, we couldn't get the chain to run out of the chain locker. So Captain Coy, calm as ever, said, "No worries, mate. One will be fine. It's strong, and it's always held in the past."

Now Captain Coy has an amazing ability to stay calm in all situations. I've never seen him get rattled in a stressful situation. So we set the anchor close to the east end of Christmas Cove, our home anchorage, with plenty of protection for the predicted northeast swell following the storm.

> We set the anchor near the east end of Christmas Cove, with plenty of protection for the swell following the storm.

We were hungry, and the seas were calm at that time, so we decided to head to one of our favorite beach bars for food and liquid confidence. Latitude 18 was a short dinghy ride across the bay and then a short drive over possibly the worst road on the entire island of St. Thomas.

Almost as soon as we arrived on the other side of the peninsula, the wind had switched around about one hundred eighty degrees. I saw that all the boats anchored were sitting just opposite of the way they normally do. That was weird. We knew that the storm had taken a more southerly route, which meant that *Gypsy Wind* was totally exposed to the waves and wind that were starting to hit.

This was not good! We ordered a dark rum and Coke and hopped back in my truck. (In the islands, it's almost a law that you drive with a drink in your hand. The standing joke is that if you get stopped by the police for talking on your cell phone while driving, they will knock $50 off the fine if you have a drink in your other hand!)

We returned to the boat, and luckily, because of her weight and the size of the anchor chain, *Gypsy Wind* had shifted position one hundred eighty degrees but hadn't started pulling the chain in the opposite direction. Her stern was no more than fifty feet from the rocky shoreline. We raised anchor, motored out further into the bay, and reset the anchor, along with a dozen or more boats in the bay.

Captain Coy then began preparing a delicious dinner out of nothing recognizable. He had an uncanny ability to make meals from the strangest combinations of food, and they always tasted great! I don't remember exactly what it was, but it probably had something to do with Rotel—canned tomatoes with green chilies with smoked oysters and wild rice.

As we ate dinner, the ocean swell began to build. By 10:00 p.m., we were bucking wildly on the anchor. Christmas Cove is a great anchorage for most Caribbean days and weather, but when the swell and wind comes from the southwest, you could not pick a more vulnerable place to anchor.

Open ocean swells from five to eight feet were now causing the boat to yank on the anchor. We were both on deck, looking back with flashlights off the stern, looking at the rocks of Great St. James Island only about seventy-five feet off the stern. It was nerve-wracking for another hour or so. Captain Coy decided to start the engine just in case the anchor gave way, and we started heading for the rocks.

After a short deliberation, we decided to pull up the anchor a second time and reset it farther out in the channel. This was no easy feat, as the rain was driving down hard, and the wind was blowing hard. It was a challenge just communicating with each other. I was on the bow running the anchor windlass, and Captain Coy was back at the helm. Captain Coy later told me that at this point, it was raining so hard he couldn't see me on the bow of the boat.

First Mate Derek Kellenbeck getting ready to entertain guests

The rain was driving down hard, and the wind was blowing hard. It was a challenge just communicating.

We reset the anchor, but our stern was still toward the rocks. We held on through howling wind, driving rain, and a growing ocean swell, and there was no sign of letting up. I went below to listen to the weather updates on the radio and check the radar, hoping to see the end of the rain bands but also hoping no other boats had broken loose from their moorings and were heading right at us.

Around midnight, the storm turned from bad to awful. We had to keep the engine running and in and out of forward gear just to keep the anchor chain from yanking on the bowsprit and possibly causing damage. The other boats around us had their running lights on as well to show other boats their positions in the bay. People were yelling and putting out rubber fenders to keep moving boats from damaging their boats.

Then boats started to drag on their anchors all around us. People were yelling and screaming trying to secure their vessels. We decided to pull the anchor and make a pitch-black run to get out of the cove and to a place of safety. Great Bay was our closest choice, but we had to maneuver through a narrow cut between two sets of rocks to get there. And it's only eighteen feet deep in the middle, giving us very little room for error.

I made my way forward to the bow in the torrential rain as the captain motored forward. Because of the growing swells, it was very slow going to get the anchor up this time. I'd get about five feet of chain in and then lose half of it back out, all while hanging on for dear life as the swells sent the bow high into the air and then down again and again.

As the anchor cleared the water, it got worse. As we slammed down into the swell, the anchor started banging back and forth against the bottom of the bowsprit. I yelled for the captain to motor forward full speed. As we turned to enter the gap through the small opening between the rocks, I stayed on the bow, still trying to get the anchor all the way up and watch to be sure we made it through.

Once we cleared the rocks, I sighed in relief and finally secured the anchor all the way snug into the bowsprit. When we turned up into Great Bay, it was as if someone had turned off a gigantic fan! As the captain was fond of saying, "The water was as calm as Hindu cows." We dropped the anchor once again, and after a couple of high fives, we made our way into our bunks without the fear of other boats ramming into us in the middle of the night, or worse, having *Gypsy Wind* crash into the rocks.

I must also add that this all took place in my first week of living aboard a sailboat. But not just any sail boat—the *Gypsy Wind* with Capt. Coy Theobalt!

Life lesson: Choose great first mates that want to learn, are avid sailors, and passionate about living their dreams.

Rum, Ribs, and Recovery

I'm sitting in the captain's quarters on *Gypsy Wind* thinking about the copious consumption of rum that took place last evening.

After we'd endured a brisk three-hour sail in cool, wet, cloudy conditions with twenty knots of sustained wind with gusts to thirty knots, all was finally good. Then one of my crew suggested that we have a little rum to celebrate a great sail under less than idyllic conditions. So I poured us a couple of stiff ones. The rationale for strong drinks is that you don't have to reload as often. I blended light rum with some dark seal rum with a splash of Coke over ice. Delightful! We sipped and talked of the sail, watched the clouds roll away, and enjoyed the beauty of a double rainbow. The sun dipped behind Red Point, and the wind began to fall off. There was a slight chill in the northerly breeze.

After a couple of drinks, it was time to think about dinner. On the menu: country-style pork ribs with wild rice perked up with broccoli, red onions, and salsa. We had another cocktail while the ribs were marinated in a concoction of every spice on the boat.

Someone turned on the music, and *Gypsy Wind* came alive with people singing and dancing in the galley. I watched the faces of newcomers as they struggled to figure out these wacky pirates. We fired up the grill, had yet another drink, and sang along with Bob Marley.

I'm not quite sure when things started getting fuzzy for me, but I think it was during dinner and had a lot to do with the large bottle of Shiraz that someone opened. It went well with the ribs, as well as to my head. After dinner, we moved to the foredeck. I lay in the hammock and pointed out constellations to the newcomers.

And so the "recovery room" is very quiet this morning. Everyone seems to have found a little spot to read or just sit and wait for the cobwebs to clear. In two hours, a family of five from Somewhere, USA, will be joining our crew. The weather has calmed and cleared, and it looks like another great day for sailing.

I'm thinking of ibuprofen and a little breakfast as well as considering giving up alcohol for Lent, which begins today. However, I may reconsider if we have a good sail that requires a celebration. We shall see.

Life lesson: Everything in moderation, including moderation.

Gypsy Wind at anchor in Christmas Cove off
the east end of St Thomas, USVI.

Steering Away from the Rocks

We are in the middle of a half-day charter. The guests have returned from snorkeling, and now the engine won't start. My mate asks me what we're going to do. I tell him that we're going sailing.

We weigh the anchor and head off on a port tack. We want to go east, but of course, that's the direction the wind is coming from. So we tack a couple of times and make our way closer to the reef that we need to negotiate to get back to the resort.

I realize that the current is pushing us off our intended course by about fifteen degrees. And the more I try to sail the boat toward the wind, the less forward headway we make and the more we get pushed off our intended course. This is not a great combination for moving through and between coral heads and rock outcroppings. But all these factors are before me, and our destination is beyond it.

In most circumstances like this, I'd fire up the "Iron Genny" (better known to landlubbers as the engine) and use the rudder to steer through the reef. But that won't be the case today.

We're told to play it safe, stay clear of danger, and learn to survive in the game of life.

Today, we do it the old-fashioned way—by the wind. I can gain a significant amount of speed by steering away from the current and off the wind a bit. However, this created unusual amounts of anxiety for everyone on board, as we had to aim directly at the rocks to get speed enough to steer around them.

Back after a day of challenging sailing, constantly having to negotiate obstacles along our route but now safely in port, I thought about this. In life, most of us are taught to "steer away from the rocks." We're told to play it safe, stay clear of danger, and learn to survive in the game of life.

I'm sure many folks reach the end of their lives without ever coming close to any rocks in their paths. Their boats are clean and have no scrapes. My life is not quite that way. I'm covered with many life scars;

most of them were due to my own stupidity or ego or whatever it is that makes a man do things he knows in his heart of hearts are not in his best interest.

As I age and (I hope) gain a measure of wisdom, I realize that we must sometimes steer consciously *toward* obstacles in order to get the momentum required to navigate around them. Without boat speed and the ability to steer left or right, I was left at the mercy of the sea. By gaining speed, I could steer *Gypsy Wind* around through the reef and into a safe harbor. No foul, no blood, no bumps against the rocks.

What obstacles are you avoiding that keep you from reaching your personal destination? It's something to think about.

Eventually, my mate discovered that the engine wouldn't start because we'd blown a couple of fan belts. It was a fairly simple fix—not too difficult on the freak-out scale. A two out of ten at best.

Now I'm heading out to talk to the owner of the water sports activity desk today to see if he might have an interest in setting up our charters for *Gypsy Wind*. This feels like a rock I must steer toward to get myself into a better position on the beach. So here I go again.

Life lesson: Sometimes we need to steer the boat of our lives toward obstacles in order to get the momentum needed to steer around them.

Part Five

Everything Changes, Everything Ends

Decisions

Here I sit, in the galley of my beloved Gypsy Wind, trying to decide whether or not to sell her.

This season has been less than good. The downturn in the economy has taken its toll on the sailing charters here in the islands. I'm tired and unsure of my next step in life. I miss friends, family, and all that comes with being at home. But I know I'll miss the ocean breeze and the sun on my face after I leave this enchanted place called the Caribbean.

I feel as though I belong here. Maybe not here on the island of St. Thomas but *here* somewhere. I get great joy from taking people sailing. I love the teaching aspect as much as the entertaining aspect. I love the feel of the wind when the boat begins to heel over and pick up speed. I love the taste of saltwater after a wave crashes over the bowsprit. I love the smells of the engine room and even the dank odor of the bilge. I love it all.

> I love the feel of the wind. I love the taste of saltwater. I love it all.

But love of the sea won't keep me on it. My love for family and friends and the tidal pull of whatever my next adventure will be at this stage of life is stronger than the call of the islands.

I know I need to end this grand experiment of trust and faith and courage and a wee bit of insanity. My loving family knows me well enough to support my adventures. Because they understand my passion about living life to the fullest, I'm allowed the gift of freedom. I'll always be grateful for that.

So I've made the decision. I'll sell *Gypsy Wind*. I've rescued her from rotting in a boatyard and brought her to her present beauty and grace. She deserved what I could give her, and I know she's thankful to me and all the friends who supported us in this endeavor. I love this boat, but it's time to release her to the winds of fate and allow another captain to experience her wonder and enchantment. I'll miss her more than I can describe.

I know beyond a shadow of a doubt that she is ready for her next adventure as well.

Life lesson: There are times in life when we must turn our backs to the wind and take a new and different path.

Sailing off Great James Island, USVI. Heading out to my favorite snorkel spot with hotel guests.

Farewell Song

Below is the last poem I wrote about my time with *Gypsy Wind*. Tears flowed from my eyes when I first penned these words.

Gypsy Wind Speaks

Go, my gypsy maiden
Go to whom you choose
May your next dance be as much fun as this one
And may your life be long on these seas
May you grace the waters where you sail
And may your admirers be drawn with awe to your beauty
I will miss you, my mistress
But we both know that every good thing must come to an end
We have grown together in many ways
Now we must go our separate ways to seek new adventures
However they may come
So go, go now, my love
Do not look back wondering about me
You will forever be in my heart
As you carry your next lover along to fulfill his dreams
Know that you will always be a part of me
May your travels take you and your crew to new lands
Filled with wonder, just as you have done for me
And may they learn to listen intently when you speak

Time to Say Good-Bye

It has been a rough road deciding to sell *Gypsy Wind*. Somewhere deep in my soul, I feel as though I am letting her down. But I also know that the time has come to say good-bye to the boat that has forever changed my life for the better.

I don't know when I realized (in my head) that the sailing business was just not making it, but it has been much longer than I knew in my heart of hearts. Some might look at this adventure and call it a failure. It hasn't been a colossal mess, but it certainly has put a strain on my relationship with my family as well as our mutual pocketbook.

When I sit back and look at this entire experience, I can't really say that I have failed. I have learned more about myself, my life, my strength and courage, and my faith than through any other experience I have attempted so far in life.

Anyway, here I am, wondering what my next adventure will be. It's the waiting that gets me hung up. I'm not good at waiting and wondering, and *Gypsy Wind* certainly taught me much about that process. I like to know what's next in the playbook of life. But I also love being carefree and footloose in some aspects of life. I'm certain that something interesting can and eventually will emerge.

Life lesson: There are times in life when we must fold up our tent, pack up our bags, and move on.
Life lesson: Everything changes, everything ends.

The End of a Great Adventure

This story—living a dream that I kept close to my heart for over forty years—did not come easily. It took blood, sweat, tears, and faith. And when I speak of faith, I am referring to faith of several kinds.

Foremost is faith in my higher power whom I choose to call God. Without a deep foundation of knowing and following this great teacher and lover of my soul, I wouldn't be here today.

Another faith is that of trusting the universe to provide all that is necessary to live a life of joy and adventure on the planet.

The third type is a faith in myself and fellow travelers in the world. I firmly believe that without faith in man's ability to take risks, reflect on his mistakes and learn from them, and then move forward toward making the planet a better place, none of this would have been possible.

My dad always said that there are three types of people—those who *make* life happen, those who *watch* life happen, and those who *wonder* what happened. I didn't understand exactly what he meant during my younger years, but as I have grown older and somewhat wiser, I am beginning to see these three types of folks more often.

Those who walk around in life in a daze wondering what happened are the "victims" of the world. They see life as something that happens *to* them without any notion that they personally participated in the outcome. These are the folks who stand at the "Please wait to be seated" sign in restaurants and, for whatever reason, get overlooked by the hostess. Rather than simply saying, "Excuse me, but we would like to be seated sometime during the next millennium," they wait, smoldering, then make a scene and stomp out the door, never to return. Victims.

Another type of victim is the one who believes that life is a series of misfortunes broken up now and then by bad luck. Not only is their glass is half-empty, but there's a crack in it. They are the whiners of the world. They are the eternal pessimists who will find eighty-four reasons why something won't work.

Then there are the guys who sit around staring at the their new watch they received at their retirement party wondering what happened for the last forty years of their lives. They went to college, worked for the corporate giant, got the watch, and are now facing retirement. They are often terrified and bewildered and swear that something happened to them over the last four decades, but they sure can't figure out what it was.

I call this group the "sideliners." These are people who never really get into the game of life. They have every excuse in the world for not becoming a player. "I hurt my knee in junior high," they say, "and the doctor told me to stay off it." They have been off those knees for thirty years.

One of my favorites is the guy who says, "I'm just too old to do that." They sit in the bleachers while others give life a try. I saw a video recently about a group of Chinese men, all over the age of eighty, who decided to recapture the excitement of their youth. They all fixed up old motorcycles and rode around the countryside for two weeks together. They got off the bench and onto the field of life.

> "There is no try, only do."
> –Yoda from *Star Wars*

The last group is comprised of folks who have decided to *make* their lives *happen*. These are the people who are willing to take risks, step out of their self-protected existence, and go for it. If they fail, at least they fail giving their all. One of the great mentors of the twentieth century, Yoda from *Star Wars*, told us, "There is no try, only do."

Yoda is right. For many years, I've been coaching people to get more engaged in the game of life. The most common response when I ask someone to commit to a new behavior is this: "I'll give it a try." My response has always been the same. I stand up, pull an empty chair to the middle of the room, and say, "Would you please try to sit in this chair?" They look at me oddly and sit down. I say, "I didn't ask you to *sit* in the chair. I asked you to *try* to sit in the chair." Eventually the lightbulb goes on. The fact is, you can't try to sit in a chair any more than you can try to get into the game of life. *There is no try, only do.* Either you suit up and get out there and give it your best, or you don't. You either do what you say you'll do, or you don't, plain and simple.

This is an interesting phenomenon in our culture today. People are unwilling to commit to things, putting decisions off as long as they can. We don't want to promise to go to someone's house for dinner after church because one of our buddies might show up at the last minute with a free ticket to the game on the fifty-yard line, in the club section, with all the free drinks and peel-and-eat shrimp you can stuff in your gullet.

I've been working very diligently for twenty years at making good on commitments—on saying yes. I don't always do it, and I'm sure that someone reading this book who knows me will certainly have at least two examples of times when I failed. But I'm moving in the right direction. I'm aware of this, and I'm working to reduce the incidence rate. At least I suited up and walked onto the field.

In *The Road Less Traveled*, M. Scott Peck says that once we agree with the reality that life is truly difficult, then life becomes easier. This guy speaks the truth, and that truth hit me squarely between the eyes many years ago.

This was the story of my life. I'd become one of those folks getting comfortable on the sidelines of life. And my life was becoming increasingly more difficult. But once I stepped off the treadmill, took stock of my life, and admitted how difficult my life had become, it started getting much easier. When I started to take responsibility for every decision I made—good, bad, or indifferent—my life took on a deeper sense of peace and easiness.

So when I decided to live a childhood dream of becoming a boat captain, I didn't just *try* to make it happen. *I made it happen.* I made decisions that eventually led me to own two sailing yachts in the U.S. Virgin Islands and start and run a sailing charter business. I accomplished all this on what my mother used to call "a wing and a prayer." I didn't know how any of this stuff would work out. If I had tried to figure everything out before I said yes, I never would have done it.

Often in life, we must close a door before a new one opens. We must step into the unknown "yes" in life and hang there in the wind with our eyes wide open until the new door opens.

With this in mind, I look back over this whole story. I had no idea where I would get a boat. But in May 2005, when I took a group of men down to the islands to sail and do a little personal reflection, I picked up a local island rag and spotted a small advertisement for a boat and business on St. Thomas. As soon as I got home, I called the number in the ad and told the owner that I was buying his boat. I also told him that I had no money, but that it would come. And it did.

Later in the summer, I flew to St. Thomas and sailed *Island Girl* with her owner, Barry Graves, to Puerto Rico. Then in November, I landed on St. Thomas, closed the sale on *Island Girl*, and started to live a dream that eventually led me to the Independent Boatyard where *Gypsy Wind* sat waiting patiently for me. *There is no try, only do.* Thanks, Yoda.

So I lift my glass high to those who make life happen—all who have gone before me as well as all who will follow. My hope is that the stories in this book help you to have the courage to live your dreams.

Here's to making your dreams coming true!

Life lesson: Get off the bench and into the game of life.
Life lesson: Say yes to life and see what happens. You will not be disappointed.

Everything changes, everything ends.

Epilogue

I actually finished writing *Gypsy Wind Speaks* about four years ago. At least I finished the content. A number of edits and rewrites have occurred since then. My life has had many curves to negotiate and hills to climb. The life lessons learned while sailing have served me well and continue to do so. And I am filled with gratitude.

During this time, I have had the opportunity to "test drive" these lessons and principles. Many of them may not be new to you, but perhaps your readiness factor is such that the timing is now right for you to launch into the next chapter of your life.

By the way, whatever you choose, life is not a bowl of cherries, as Erma Bombeck often said. Life is not always and, I am finding, rarely "easy" in the traditional sense of the word. But life is worth living no matter how challenging it becomes, if your interest level is learning more than in acquiring more.

The road less traveled is so because it's not easy. I often tell folks living fully is not for the faint of heart. It's a long, challenging journey no matter how you slice it. The key or at least one of the keys in living fully is in a person's attitude.

My hope is that this tale of adventure, mishaps, and success in some ways inspires you to sit down and take a long look at your life. Do you have what you want in life or not? If you do, then dance the night away and get up tomorrow and set your sails for new horizons.

If you do not have what you want, I invite you to take some time to ponder your situation. I have created a process to follow if you are interested. It is nothing more than a condensed version of all the life lessons that I follow today to negotiate the waters of life. My hope is that these mile posts will help you along your journey.

Here is my final toast to you:

May the sun rise up to greet you.
May the wind be always at your back.
May you find a measure of happiness in all your endeavors.
And may you find yourself sliding into your grave at the end, saying,
"That was one hell of a ride!"

The Four Amigos: Derek Kellenbeck blowing the conch, Paul Drda, Jordan
Barrows, and me. Without these great men to encourage me, challenge
me, and support me, I would not have written this book. Thanks mates!!

Appendix A

Gypsy Wind

SPEC SHEET

Builder
– Formosa Boat Builders, Taipei, Taiwan, 1979.

Length
– 57 feet overall.

Beam
– 14 feet 6 inches.

Gross tonnage
– 53,000 pounds.

Water
– 485 gallons in Stainless Steel (6 tanks) New Force 10-6 gal hot water installed (4/08). Two freshwater pumps mounted side by side. When one goes out, you can switch to the other in less than five minutes.

Fuel
– 260 gallons diesel (three steel tanks).

Generator
- Northern Lights 8 KW (6,800 hours) new saltwater pump (4/08). New freshwater impeller (7/06).

Engine
- Perkins T6.354.4 M (120 horsepower) rebuilt 7/06, < 250 hours run time. All gauges are VDO and could use upgrading but are fully functional.

Drive Train
- Velvet Drive transmission on 2-inch shaft leading to 26-inch bronze 3-blade propeller.

Bilge Pumps
- Two Rule high output electric pumps with spare backup.
- One Gusher hand pump very conveniently located.

Water Maker
- Yes, but I have never used it. Not sure if it works. Previous owner claimed 37 gallons per hour.

Electrical System
- 110 from generator and shore power, 12-volt house system with two new D3 batteries (12/07), 24 volts for windlass and some house lighting, 4 new golf cart batteries (3/08). I love them. The boat has Phase 3—24-volt and 12-volt chargers. Heart interface charger/ inverter.

Navigation
1. New Standard Horizons Chart plotter (1/08) with chip for Venezuela to Southern Florida, all of Caribbean, Mexico, and Central America.
2. New Standard Horizons VHF with loudspeaker capabilities (1/07).
3. New Standard Horizons RAM microphone for helm (1/07).
4. Furuno Radar.
5. Data Marine speed/depth.

6. Data Marine wind indicator.
7. Simrad/Robertson Auto Pilot—currently not working.
8. Handheld Garman GPS (new in 2006).

Rigging
– All standing rigging has been upgraded to 5/16-inch or 1/4-inch stainless 7x9 aircraft cable with Stalock fastening system. The stanchions are 42 feet high custom made 1 and 1/14 inch 316 stainless. The three rows of lifelines are 1/4-inch 7x9 stainless. All the standing rigging attachment plates on the masts were replaced with custom made 316 stainless (12/06). The after spreaders were replaced with aged spruce (12/06). The main mast spreaders were removed repainted and sealed (12/06). There are enough Stalock spares to completely redo the boat if ever needed.

Sail Inventory
– A mix of old and new. The Mainsail was new in 2004 and was hoisted only three times in three years. The spinnaker looks like it has never been out of the bag. Condition unknown. The genoa is okay. It needs some cosmetic stitching, but the sailcloth is good. The mizzen is tired. It needs replacing. The Yankee looks new. I have never used it. The staysail is in good shape.

Sailing Hardware
– Pro Furl roller furling on both foresails. All main winches have been upgraded to Lewmar self-tailing. The boat has three 40s, two 54s, and one 50. The other five are a combination of Custom Yachts and Barlow. They are all in perfect working condition. The jib sheets were replaced with Kevlar 12 MM line (1/07). All rigging was inspected, and all recommendations were done to the riggers specs on (12/06). Both masts are original and in good condition according to the rigger. However, they were painted at some point in the past by the previous owner, and it makes it difficult to be precise on their condition.

Dinghy

– None, but it does have a Yamaha 15 Enduro (new in 04, < 20 hours run time). Edsen Davit system on stern (easily hoists a 12 feet long dinghy)

Grill
– Magma Avalon. Two-burner stainless steel with two 7.5-pound propane tanks.

Topsides
– New Awlgrip sprayed on 9/07

Bottom paint
– New antifouling paint 12/07

Deck
– Teak was removed in 1999 and fiber-glassed. New surface applied 2/08 (two-part acrylic paint with nonskid)

Pilot House
– Painted 2/08

Anchors
– One 110-pound plow with 300 feet of 1/2-inch BB chain
– One 85-pound plow with 300 feet of 1/3-inch BB chain.
– One Aluminum Danforth stern anchor with 30 feet of 3/8-inch chain and 300 feet of 5/8-inch line.

Windlass
– LoFrans Titan – 2,400 pounds of pulling strength. Both forward anchors operate off this windlass. It also has a cat head which can come in very handy at times.

Forward
– High pressure freshwater deck rinse, also high pressure saltwater deck rinse.

Four deck boxes
– Eight life jackets
– Extra lines and six 1-inch braided dock lines (7/06)

- Air conditioner, spare diesel fuel can, numerous tarps
- Numerous snorkel and dive gear: two tanks, BCD, and regulator included

Life raft
- Has not been serviced in a number of years. Deck mounted on pilot house with hydrostatic release mechanism. I cannot comment on its condition.

Helm
- Teak flooring covered with elastomeric roofing finish with nonskid (2/08). Classic compass. Traditional wheel.

Pilot House
- Galley and dining. Force 10 Princess three-burner stove with oven that actually works! Comes with two 20-pound propane tanks mounted under seat on deck just forward of pilot house. Gold Star microwave oven. Double stainless sink, complete set of pots and pans, as well as cutlery, plates, and glassware.

Fridge and freezer
- Sea Frost cold plates. This is a 110-volt system. It has a saltwater cooling pump and runs on R12 refrigerant.

Entertainment
- Sony 10-CD changer with Sony AM/FM/CD player.
- Panasonic 13-inch color TV with powered antenna.
- Aspire digital DVD player.
- Yamaha Stereo Receiver (110 Volt), great when using shore power.
- Sony speakers in saloon, West Marine speakers at helm, Acoustic Marine speaker for deck sound (1/08), and an extra pair of KLH speakers for wherever you want them.

Heads
- Forward has a classic Blakes Lavac toilet, completely rebuilt 12/07.

– Aft head is a Jabsco. I replaced the complete pump system for it in 1/08. Both sinks in heads are original stainless and in great condition.

Miscellaneous

– This boat has an electric oil pump out for changing engine oil that is very handy. It has spare parts beyond imagination. There is a thousand-dollar stainless for running rigging. There are at least one or more replacements pumps for every pump on the boat. There is a spare compressor for the fridge/freezer. There are several filters and belts for every need. It also has a new HP color printer (3/08). The pilot house has a Weems and Plath brass barometer and 12-hour and unique 24-hour clocks.

Appendix B

Life Lessons from a Sailboat

Speak less, listen more.

Slow down, relax, and take time when maneuvering in tight places.

Sometimes you have to play by the local rules to get what you need, even if it goes against your ethics.

Persistence pays off!

Appreciate friends.

Learn to enjoy being alone without being lonely.

Relationship before business, always.

Slow down, breathe, and focus on the present.

Don't just do something; sit there.

Learn to breathe into life and start to "be" versus "do."

Admit mistakes quickly without assigning blame or judgment.

When in doubt about what to do, stop, breathe, relax, and prioritize what needs to be done.

Trust your gut about your future and don't let obstacles deter you from your dreams.

Taking stock and personal inventory of life is essential to healthy living.

If you are going to make changes, make sure you do your homework first.

Persistence pays off.

Always invite your friends to share in your excitement about something.

When you have "rats" on your "boat," make sure you do whatever necessary to eliminate them.

Persistence often pays off, especially when combined with compassion.

Sometimes we must change our course to get to the destination.

Don't put off doing what needs to be done. Face the difficulties in life and address them.

Look everywhere for life teachers. You will find them if you only will look.

Stay present. Live in the here and now rather than in a fantasy world about the future.

Be open to what life is trying to teach us at every turn.

Do less, be more. Allow the student to learn instead of trying to "teach."

Check your ego at the door when teaching others.

Don't drink to excess, especially cheap tequila.

Take time to enjoy yourself on a regular basis. Spend a day acting like a tourist.

Take advantage of local knowledge when dealing with governmental issues.

Don't take shortcuts.

Most major problems begin with a series of minor problems.

Keep your wits about you when you are in a dangerous situation.

The same thinking that caused a problem cannot be used to solve it.

When life-changing events occur, take time to listen to what the event is telling you.

Do what needs to be done, no matter how it impacts your ego.

Sometimes it's best to stop our forward movement and take stock of the present situation.

Slow down and take time to enjoy the simple things, like the sunsets, the gardens growing, the wind in the trees, and the clouds high in the sky.

Don't agree to do something you already know ahead of time you will not do.

When under stress, breathe, stay present, and deal with all the "shoulds" that are in your head.

My problems are not near as large as I think they are in the grand scheme of life.

Life is made up of a huge number of choices we make. The better choices we make, the better life we have.

Slow down, breathe, and take time to smell the daffodils.

Start asking yourself better questions.

Recognize that when we start telling ourselves when something "should" happen, we have slipped into thinking that the universe revolves around us.

Take time to appreciate the simple things in life.

Learn to lean into and live your purpose on planet Earth.

Figure out what you really want in life and go after it.

Take time to drive down the backroads of life.

Take time to drive down some of the side roads in life. Make a list of everything that needs to be done and then check them off when each is done.

Pay attention to your inward state of being. If you need help, get it.

Take stock of your emotional state on a regular basis.

When you need help, ask for it!

Recognize when you are using old ways of coping that are no longer working for you and develop healthier ones.

Lean into your fear and use it to free you from its grip and control.

Take time to allow nature to teach you lessons that you need to learn.

With every dream, there are nightmares along the way.

Dare to dream. For without dreams, we are merely spectators in the game of life.

Find someone that can encourage and support you when you are feeling down and out or just lazy.

An attitude of gratitude is the key to happiness.

Choose great first mates that want to learn, are avid sailors, and passionate about living their dreams.

Everything in moderation, including moderation.

Sometimes we need to steer the boat of our lives toward obstacles in order to get the momentum needed to steer around them.

There are times in life when we must turn our backs to the wind and take a new and different path.

There are times in life when we must fold up our tent, pack up our bags, and move on.

Everything changes, everything ends.

Get off the bench and into the game of life.

Say yes to life and see what happens. You will not be disappointed.

Made in United States
North Haven, CT
12 December 2023